ESSENTIAL RIDING

ESSENTIAL
RIDING

A REALISTIC APPROACH TO HORSEMANSHIP

Steven D. Price

The Lyons Press

All photographs, unless otherwise specified, are by Werner Rentsch

Printed in Canada

10 9 8 7 6 5 4 3 2

Library of Congress Cataloging-in-Publication Data
Price, Steven D.
    Essential Riding: a realistic approach to horsemanship/Steven D. Price
    p. cm.
    ISBN 1-58574-002-0
    1. Horsemanship. I. Title.
SF309.P838 2000
798.2'3—dc21

                                                      00-024119

Riding is simple . . . it's just not easy.
—Anonymous

A perfect book on riding could be written only by a horse.
—Vladimir S. Littauer

CONTENTS

INTRODUCTION

I am not an expert in horses and do not speak with assurance.
I can always tell which is the front end of a horse, but beyond
that my art is not above the ordinary.
—Mark Twain, *A Biography*

My first riding lesson might well have turned out to be my last one.

I was 11 years old and spending my first summer at Camp Taconic in western Massachusetts. A few days after camp opened, I joined four of my bunkmates at the riding ring. The instructor, an imposing, ruddy-complexioned local farmer named Moe, waited there for us. So did six horses. Three had English saddles, the others Western ones.

All the horses had been at camp before. So had my bunkmates, who spent much of the walk up to the ring deciding who would ride whom. I was left with Blue Jay, a chunky blue roan with by-no-means exclusive Quarter Horse ancestry.

When Moe told us to get our horses, I didn't hesitate. Lots of time at amusement park pony rides had taught me the rudiments of mounting (with which the horn on Blue Jay's Western saddle helped immeasurably) and how to hold the reins. With typical pre-adolescent reticence in new situations, I said nothing about it being my first riding lesson when Moe walked over to adjust my stirrups.

Moe climbed on his horse, Colonel, a huge chestnut five-gaited Saddlebred, and surveyed the group. "Bring Blue Jay up behind me," he told me. As if programmed to obey Moe, Blue Jay took his place.

We walked past the riding ring and down a trail toward the lake. "Lines up, heels down, and trot," Moe turned and told us, and off we went. In front of me, Moe rose out of and then sank back into the saddle at every stride. "That's posting," I told myself, for I had read a book. Bouncing and trying to stay on board, I tried to post. Again the saddle horn came to my rescue.

Down at the lake was a small beach. When we walked our horses into the water, I saw how the others let the reins slip through their fingers until their horses were able to drink. I did it, too. Moe looked over at me and winked. I grinned back. This riding business didn't seem hard at all.

The trail continued toward an unpaved county road. "Yea! Agony Hill!" my bunkmates cheered. "Stay together," Moe instructed.

We turned left onto the road. Ahead lay a long, straight uphill stretch. Colonel pranced in anticipation, and Blue Jay seemed to tense up. Looking over his shoulder, Moe told us, "Okay, boys, lines up, heels down—and catch me if you can!"

Colonel took off. So did all the other horses. Thrown back into the saddle, I braced one hand against the horn and considered my situation. I was the veteran of enough cowboy movies to know we were cantering—if not galloping. But that was all I knew. Neither my pony rides nor the book I'd read had offered any insights about what I should be doing.

The road beneath Blue Jay's feet flew by. So did rocks and gravel that Colonel's hooves kicked up.

In moments of crisis, all we can do is what we know. All I knew about riding at anything faster than a walk was to post. And so, as Blue Jay bounded along, I did my best to stand up and down in the stirrups. Or maybe it was just bouncing—I didn't analyze technique at the time.

At the top of the hill, Moe raised a hand to signal a halt. Colonel stopped. So did my bunkmates' horses. Blue Jay kept going.

With my reins too long to be effective, Blue Jay swerved around Colonel and continued down the road. He didn't get far, though. Moe spurred Colonel after him and, within a few strides, reached over and grabbed one of Blue Jay's reins.

Once we had stopped, the instructor (in retrospect, I couldn't consider him *my* instructor yet) glared at me. "What the hell were you doing?" His ruddy face became even redder. "Why didn't you stop your horse?"

No good answer came to my mind. All I could do was shrug.

"Well, why didn't you stop him?" Moe continued. "You know how to ride."

I saw my opening. "Actually, I don't," I said tentatively.

"Of course you do. You've been riding here—how many years is it now?"

"Actually, this is my first summer here."

"Come on, you've been coming to Taconic for a couple of years."

Now I was on firmer ground. "No. I promise. This is my first time here. And I've never had riding lessons."

Moe's complexion went from ruddy to ashen. "You're . . . ?"

"Steve. Steve Price."

"Well, Steven," Moe glanced around at my bunkmates, then lowered his voice. "Let's keep this our little secret."

Despite that inauspicious beginning, I went back for more. Moe taught me when posting was appropriate and when it wasn't, along with other basics of "survival-seat equitation," as I later came to describe his brand of instruction. And I went home with the knowledge that riding lessons are a Very Good Thing.

The more I rode at camp over subsequent summers, the more I came to enjoy the sport. Every free moment was spent at the ring importuning Moe for "free rides" whenever a spare horse was available. And whenever possible, I watched him teach, the beginning of my love affair with riding lessons.

I also rode during winter months. The year I entered high school, I joined the riding club. It had many benefits: The stable where the club met offered more sophisticated instruction than Moe did; moreover, like Fort

Lauderdale during spring breaks of that era, the club and the stable were where the girls were. Cosi and John Napolitano, the two brothers who owned the stable, were active members of the area's horse-show community. Through them, I discovered the competitive side of equestrian life. That was during the 1950s, the "good old days" when the only limit to the heights of jumper fences was the amount of available lumber and when, at outdoor shows, night classes were illuminated by the headlights of cars pointed into the ring (I hasten to add that I was strictly a spectator).

Our high school riding club's annual trip to the National Horse Show at Madison Square Garden introduced me to competition at the highest levels. The Irish, Mexican, and other international squads rode against the U.S. Equestrian Team, the horses and riders doing things that lessons on school horses could only hint at. There was a big world out there and, although I knew I'd never soar over big fences on such horses, I kept on riding. I kept on reading, too, discovering the vast wealth of equestrian lore that was available no farther away than the local library or the bookshelves of tack shops and friends.

A few years later, when I was in college, I approached Moe about a summer job. He supplied horses and instructors to a number of camps throughout the Berkshires, one of which was down the road from Camp Taconic. By happy coincidence, Camp Lenore needed an instructor. In the greatest miracle of animal survival since Noah's Ark weathered the Flood, the six camp horses, the campers who took riding, and one fledgling instructor all made it unscathed through the summer.

I kept on riding. When I moved to New York City after college and graduate school, Central Park's bridle paths beckoned. So did trails served by suburban stables. Vacations at equestrian resorts were yet another, more concentrated opportunity to ride and take lessons.

Whenever people asked, "Why continue to take lessons?—you know how to ride," my answer came easily. Golfers routinely take lessons from their club pro. Tennis players attend instructional clinics. Professional baseball teams have pitching, batting, and fielding coaches to help their players avoid bad habits or to correct them. And if Olympic-caliber U.S. Equestrian Team riders work with coaches, who was I to say I knew enough? It wasn't being smug or self-effacing to admit that the more I watched good riders, the more I realized how little I knew.

In the course of almost three decades of writing about horses—and even earlier—I've had the opportunity for formal instruction or just an occasional tip from some of the world's best horsemen and horsewomen. Alas, if only I were as good a rider as they've been teachers. Also in course of writing about horses, I've read a great deal about riding and especially about learning how to ride. And I've learned a considerable amount from books and magazines, from basic manuals to more sophisticated and more technical works.

Basic how-to-ride manuals present a particular problem. No matter how eminent the author or how clearly he or she describes the learning process, the books are predicated on the reader's learning on a well-trained horse. "Do this, this, and that," the book instructs, "and your horse will respond in such-and-such a way." The implication is that simply pushing the right buttons will make any horse canter on the correct lead or halt in a smooth and balanced fashion or otherwise behave like the well-schooled animals that the author no doubt rides. In the magic world of these manuals, nothing ever goes wrong.

Unfortunately, that isn't how the real world works. The vast majority of us learn to ride on lesson horses at public stables or on privately owned "backyard" horses. Even if they were well trained in their prime, they've seen better days. Moreover, they've become inured to being lesson horses. When the beginning rider does "this, this, and that," the horse is just as likely to respond with no more than a yawn.

For instance, a rider may apply certain rein and leg cues that "the book" says will produce a flawless canter departure. But they don't—nothing happens. The only way to get old Pokey to canter, the rider quickly learns, is to trot him into the gait, kicking like mad and clucking like a demented chicken while everyone standing along the ring's rail yells, "Canter, Pokey, canter!"

The result are feelings of frustration and of unfairness, too. Beginners can't be expected to know enough to be able to determine how much of an incorrect response or no response is their fault and how much is their horse's, so they tend to blame themselves at times when they shouldn't. Even instructors with the best will in the world can't be expected to heap too much blame on the horse, since the quality of the horse's training is usually considered a reflection of the instructor or trainer.

The purpose of this book is to provide a real-world perspective for you as a beginning rider. As you'll discover, sometimes a problem is of your own making, but sometimes it's the horse's fault. Knowing how to distinguish between the two will make a big difference in your equestrian education. So will learning how to cope with and correct an errant animal, and learning when to let a more experienced person take over the chore.

Essential Riding is not a book for people who plan to learn to ride on their own. As I'll elaborate in the first chapter, if you approach the sport with a book in one hand and a horse in the other, you'll have your hands full in more ways than one. Instead, this book will help you find a suitable instructor—and horse—and then understand the whys and wherefores of what your instructor is saying and what you're doing. The more you understand, the faster you'll learn and the better you'll appreciate the subtleties of horsemanship.

As the word *essential* implies, this primer is intended to introduce you to the sport. When you've finished, you'll have learned the basic rider position; the basic gaits of the walk, trot, and canter (or for you Western riders, the walk, jog, and lope); how to enjoy a safe trail ride; and, for those of you interested in jumping, the basics of form over fences. Later chapters deal with the range of horse sports you might want to explore, horseback vacations, and sources of further information.

People, including authors, can sing the praises of horseback riding to the heavens, but the best way to realize the truth of their words is to see for yourself. You're off to a sensible start, or else you wouldn't be reading a book about learning to ride. The rest is up to you.

Happy trails!
Steve Price

ACKNOWLEDGMENTS

Whether as teachers, riding companions, or colleagues, the following people have heightened my appreciation of horses and horsemanship. My gratitude is boundless.

Maurice "Moe" O'Connell, John and Cosimo Napolitano, Joe Vanorio, Anthony and Michael D'Ambrosio, Harry Case, Fred Brill, Barbara Burn, Gail and Werner Rentch, Jean Walker, Alix Coleman, Marilyn and Alex Mackay-Smith, Caroline Treviranus, Michael O. Page, Armand Leone, Ronnie Mutch, Mark Leone, George H. Morris, Bill Steinkraus, Lily and Jean Froissard, Mary Jane Mitchell, Joan Hansen, Linda Levine, Liz Dickmann, Anne Kofod, Jane Grenci Azznara, Mandy Lorraine, Rita Grenci, Carol and Ray Molony, Ann Grenci, Joe Lynam, Kim Jacobs, Scot Evans, Don Burt, Amy and Jerry O'Connor, Lori Rakoczy, Katie Hollander, Ric Pinckney,

Boots and Dave Wright, Fred Sagarin, Lesli K. Groves, Leslie Miller, Carol Ellis, and Sarah Cotton.

Among the horses along the way: Blue Jay, High Hat, Belle Starr, Maverick, Casper, All Aboard, Henry, Bubby, Alvin, Fonty, Driftwood, and especially Riviera City and Mighty Manfred.

Special thanks to Werner Rentsch and Amy Warnick (and Higgins and Waldo) for taking and posing for many of the photographs, respectively. And to my editors Lilly Golden and Enrica Gadler.

Profound gratitude to Barbara Cochrane, Anne L. W. Price, Kip Rosenthal, and Myron Weiss.

I

LEARNING TO RIDE

Natural talent, no matter how great, can't make up for a
lack of basic knowledge and skills.
—Anne Kursinski, *Anne Kursinski's
Riding and Jumping Clinic*

One of the great mysteries of this life is why people who would never dream of getting behind the wheel of a car or strapping on a pair of skis without proper instruction don't think twice about getting on a horse without first learning how to ride.

Perhaps it's because riding looks so easy. Posses in westerns and cavalry charges in costume drama movies were full of people who hopped into the saddle and galloped off, suffering nothing worse than a bullet or arrow wound or a slash from a saber.

But life isn't the movies. Riding is a skill that's acquired through instruction. It's also a sport in which the equipment includes another living creature. A large creature at that, one that's 10 times heavier and stronger than his rider.

Safety is thus as much a factor in riding as it is in driving, skiing, or any other potentially hazardous activity. And the safest, as well as the most efficient, way to learn is on a trustworthy horse under the supervision of a knowledgeable and sympathetic instructor.

LESSON STABLES

Many, if not most people learn to ride from professional instructors. Although not all stables offer beginner lessons (some places cater only to more advanced riders who own their own horses), finding a suitable facility won't be very difficult. Word of mouth is a good start. A friend, relative, or neighbor who rides may be able to recommend a place. The proprietor or a clerk at a local saddlery shop (or tack shop) will certainly know about a barn that teaches beginners (the words *stable* and *barn* are used interchangeably in common usage). Also to be found in the classified section of your phone book, under RIDING ACADEMIES or HORSEBACK RIDING, are names and addresses of the stables themselves.

Once you've learned of a place, phone to say you'd like to go out and look around. Arrange a time when you can spend a few minutes with the barn manager or a senior instructor. Ask about a time when you can also observe a private or group beginner lesson.

Taking along a friend or relative who rides is a good idea, although not absolutely essential. You may barely know which end of the horse gets the carrot, but your common sense can tell when a stable looks like a good place for your purposes.

The first question to ask the manager or another staff member is whether the place offers the kind of riding you'll want to do: English or Western, riding only in a ring (or *arena*, the Western and dressage term), or on trails, or both. If jumping, dressage, or another English-style discipline appeals to you, you'll want a barn that teaches that technique. If your riding career is likely to include reining or other Western pursuits, that's the emphasis you'll want in the barn you choose.

Scheduling is always an issue, especially for youngsters in school or working adults. Can you take lessons at times that are good for you? Is there an indoor arena where you can ride when the weather's too cold or wet for outdoor activities?

Some people learn better with one-on-one instruction. Others prefer group lessons. That's up to you and the barn's policy. Cost is also a factor: Private lessons are more expensive than semiprivate (the term for two or three students in the class), which, in turn, are more expensive than group lessons. The price of private and group lessons varies widely from barn to barn, and that's the *only* definitive statement I can make about the cost of riding lessons.

If you're concerned about the cost of continuing private lessons, you might consider starting with a few such lessons until you get the rudiments down. Then switch to group sessions.

An informal stroll through the barn will give you a good idea about how the operation is run. Among the questions to consider is whether the horses look well cared for, with clean stalls and bedding material and water buckets that are filled. The aisles should be swept free of manure and bedding, with no rakes, brooms, or other tools lying on the floor waiting for an accident to happen. A rule of thumb is that good instructors seldom choose to work at stables that don't take good care of the health and safety of their employees, both the equine and human varieties.

Watching a lesson will tell you a great deal about a barn. Because advanced riding involves subtle and sophisticated techniques that the uninitiated will find difficult to follow, you're better off observing a lesson at the beginner or beginner-intermediate level.

You've been in enough teaching or learning situations in your life to know when you're watching a good lesson. Is the instructor taking an active interest in the student(s) or does he or she seem to be just going through the motions? Instructors who sit on the rail and chat with colleagues or stare off into space instead of focusing on the horse and rider win no prizes for pedagogy. Neither do instructors who yell and scream. Riding has its potential physical dangers and there are times when a sharp command may avert an accident, but leather-lunged instructors who constantly berate and humiliate recruits went out with the horse cavalry . . . or should have.

You will notice that horses used in beginner lessons bear little resemblance to the spirited steeds found at racetracks or horse shows. That's as it should be. No one takes driving lessons in a Ferrari or a

Richard Petty Daytona 500 special. By the same token, no one learns to ride on a top show-quality animal. What you're looking at is a species known as the Lesson Horse.

Lesson (or school) horses come in a variety of sizes, shapes, and colors. They also comes in a variety of breeds, although most are cross-breeds or the equine equilvalent of mutts, known as *grades.*

Whatever he looks like, the lesson horse occupies a very special niche in the order of things. Part saint, part bureaucrat, part caretaker, and part heartbreaker, he's seen it all. And he's done it all, too, although "having it done to him" is more accurate. Beginners bounce on his back, yank on his mouth, and kick his sides. They give the horse conflicting signals and then become upset when he fails to read their mind and do the one thing they want him to do. A school horse that's used for beginner jumping lessons is often caught in the mouth by the rider's hands (via the reins) when he leaves the ground and again when he lands.

The workday life of a school horse is full of ups and downs. The first lesson of the day may be spent toting a rank beginner (and all that job involves). His next lesson may involve a more educated rider, but the one after that might be a trail ride under someone who wants to "get his money's worth" by nonstop galloping.

It's no wonder that lesson horses have more defense mechanisms than a Psychology 101 textbook. Their most prevalent response is to work as little as possible. Given the chance, a lesson horse will walk instead of trotting or trot instead of cantering. Or he'll stop instead of going forward. Given the opportunity to duck into the center of the ring and doze in the sun, that's what'll he do. It's not just laziness that causes this behavior: Lesson horses quickly learn to test a rider by seeing how much they can get away with (the analogy to bureaucrats who've figured out how to work the system is most appropriate).

But don't feel too sorry for lesson horses. They're valued employees of any barn. As such they're well fed and well cared for, because they can be counted on to earn their keep and then some. In his own way, a lesson horse is as valuable as the most successful show horse in the barn.

LEARNING TO RIDE FROM A FRIEND— AND ON A FRIEND'S HORSE

A horse-owning friend or neighbor who's encouraging you to learn to ride may nevertheless be unwilling to let you learn on his or her animal. That reluctance is perfectly reasonable. The horse may be specially trained for competition or simply too much horse for a beginner. On the theory that "you don't learn to drive in a Ferrari," the owner doesn't want to see the animal spoiled or you injured.

However, that person may have another horse that would be perfect for your purposes. Or someone else might. The world is full of backyard pleasure mounts, some of which are retired show horses that have slowed down over the years. If that's the case, the owner may have the necessary interest, time, patience, and expertise to be your instructor. Or there may be a member of the family or a friend who fits that category.

Not just any rider makes a good instructor. Many "natural" riders who are great on a horse haven't a clue about what they're doing. You'll want someone who knows about riding and has the ability to convey that knowledge.

There's much to recommend this kind of lesson arrangement. First of all, it'll be a one-on-one learning situation, which tends to be the most rewarding. Then, too, you'll be the only novice who'll ride the horse, and the owner or instructor can easily reschool the animal before any bad school-horse habits become ingrained.

Access to a riding ring or arena is a definite plus. The ring needn't be very large or the fencing very high, but being enclosed helps keep a horse's attention focused on the job at hand. It keeps the rest of him, with you on his back, from wandering off, too.

With regard to the cost of such lessons, the owner or youngster or friend may be happy to teach you as a favor. You should certainly offer to pay, though.

An alternative mode of payment is barter: You can help clean out stalls and perform other barn chores. That's also an excellent way to develop a knowledge of horses and horsekeeping that will enhance your understanding and appreciation of the sport.

2

UNDERSTANDING HORSES

After a certain point, our sport is about 90% horse and
how you can learn to adapt to that horse.
>   —Norman dello Joio, *Riding for America*

The one accurate generalization on the subject of horses is there are no easy generalizations. Horses are individuals, each with his own idiosyncratic personality. However, certain instincts and behaviors that are common to all members of the species will shed light on their behavior. Knowing about them is useful because you can use many to your advantage. (On the other hand, other instincts and behaviors tend to interfere with the riding process, although you'll eventually be able to minimize their effects.)

Physical features as well as behavior patterns help explain how and why horses act and react as they do. That's why, before we get to behavior, we'll start with an overview of how a horse is constructed. Besides, once you learn the terms for the various parts of the horse, you'll more easily understand what instructors and other riders are talking about.

Let's start at the bottom.

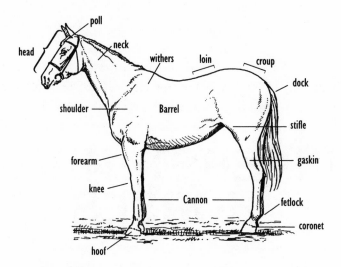

The parts of the horse

The hard wall that surrounds the foot is the *hoof.* Like human fingernails, hooves grow and, therefore, must be trimmed periodically. Blacksmiths (also called farriers) will do that chore in conjunction with shoeing. Horses need metal shoes because as solid as hooves are, rocks and roads are harder.

The soft triangle on the bottom of the foot is called the *frog,* which is protected by the hoof wall and the horseshoe.

The hoof and the foot come together at a place called the *coronet.* Above the coronet is the *fetlock,* which flexes the way your wrist does.

Each foreleg has two long bones—the *forearm* and the *cannon*—that meet at the *knee.*

The bones of the hind legs are the *gaskin* and the *cannon.* They meet at the *hock,* which is the equivalent of the human elbow.

The gaskin connects to the body at a joint called the *stifle.* It works the way your hip does.

The hard little calluslike lump on the inside of each lower leg is the *chestnut.* These are as distinctive in shape and texture as fingerprints; in fact, they're used to verify identification in horse racing and in registering foals in certain breed registries.

Like Caesar's Gaul, a horse's body is divided into three parts. Starting from the back, the *hindquarters* are made up of the *loin* and the *croup.*

The top of the tail is called the *dock.* Its muscle lets the horse swish his tail not only to shoo away flies but also to indicate displeasure.

The middle part of the horse's body is called the *barrel.*

The *forehand* is in front of the barrel. The highest point of the body, where the neck joins the body, is the *withers.* Height is measured from the withers down to the ground in units called *hands.* Each hand is 4 inches, so a horse that measures 62 inches from his withers to the ground is said to stand 15.2 hands high.

The *forelegs* join the body at the *shoulder.*

The horse's long, flexible *neck* lets him reach down to graze on grass and reach up to browse from trees. The neck also acts to balance his relatively heavy *head* while he moves.

The highest point of the horse, the spot between his ears, is called the *poll.*

Like other animals with long funnel-shaped ears, horses have an acute sense of hearing. They pick up sounds by turning one or both ears in any direction, much the way satellite dishes work.

You'll learn to keep an eye on a horse's ears, because they're often an indication of his attitude. Ears pricked forward show an interest in something ahead. Both ears flattened against the head is a sign of anger.

Horses have the largest eyes of any land animal. Set back on either side of the head, the eyes offer a panoramic range of almost 360 degrees (the exception is directly behind the horse). However, having eyes that are set so far apart creates a blind spot in front of the horse's face and under his nose. The only way he can see anything there is by lifting or turning his head.

Horses have *monocular* vision, which means they register things with only one eye at a time; the brain then sorts out and coordinates the image from each eye. Lacking the binocular vision that we have, a horse has virtually no depth perception. Turning his head when he nears an object is how he gauges the distance (this becomes crucial when approaching a jump).

Horses perceive objects as larger than they really are. Humans appear 9 or 10 feet tall to them, which may be why they obey us giants.

A horse's eyes become accustomed to changes in light much more slowly than our eyes do. An animal's response to moving from dark shadows to bright sunshine or vice versa is caution; some horses will stop and stand stock still when coming out of a dark barn into the sunshine. Let them adjust to the change before moving on.

Large nostrils help give a horse an acute sense of smell. The moment a horse picks up an unfamiliar odor, instinct takes over and he tries to determine whether the smell is coming from a friend or a foe. Because this sense is so important to horses, they become anxious on windy days. They toss and fuss with their heads as if trying to receive smells.

A horse's teeth come in at different ages, and some change their shape over time (hence the expression *long in the tooth* for someone who's getting on in years). Knowledgeable horsemen and horsewomen are able to estimate a horse's age with a high degree of accuracy by examining the size and shape of the teeth.

The equine sense of touch refers more to being touched than doing the touching. Horses are able to feel the slightest pressure on their skin, as you'll see when they nip or kick at even tiny insects that buzz around or land on them.

EQUINE BEHAVIOR

Humans aren't the only species that likes horses. Wolves, coyotes, and mountain lions also like them, but for a different reason.

Having spent millions of years worrying about ending up as another creature's dinner, horses just can't seem to get the "they're out to get me" attitude out of their collective subconscious. Whenever something—make that *anything*—frightens a horse, his knee-jerk reaction is to get away. Sometimes his response takes the form of shying—just a little "spook" at something in the road. Or he may make a few terrified strides before he calms down. In the most extreme cases, he'll bolt and run away.

In other words, horses scoot first and then ask questions, and *any* horse, including the oldest, most placid, bombproof school horse, has the physical and emotional resources to become upset over a real or imagined danger. Don't ever forget that fact.

Horses enjoy the company of other horses. They feel safe being part of a herd because there's safety in numbers. That herd instinct becomes apparent in a group lesson or on a trail ride with other horses. A horse—especially a school horse—that's asked to leave the group (he'd call it a herd) will be reluctant to leave. He'll balk and, when finally urged away by his rider, he'll look back and often voice his separation anxiety with a

As a herd animal, a horse is more comfortable out on a trail ride in the company of others. Even one other horse constitutes a "mini-herd."

11

whinny. On the other hand, the same horse will move faster—on his own—to rejoin the group.

Although horses enjoy the company of others, they're not always happy to be in close proximity. Even school horses that are accustomed to going head to tail may suddenly decide to object to a neighbor. Danger signals include ears laid back, widened eyes, and bared teeth. Whether you're riding the aggressor or the victim, you'll want to move your horse out of harm's way as fast as you can; separating the belligerents by a couple of lengths will defuse the situation. And if you're on the ground, don't try to play peacemaker—just get out of the way.

Akin to a horse's bucking or kicking out of displeasure is the playful snort or buck that comes from "feeling his oats." As playful as it might be, a little "feelin' good" crow-hop can still dislodge an unwary rider. Even when you're mounted on a senior citizen, be especially alert on the first few cool days after a warm spell or whenever a brisk breeze is blowing.

Whether a horse lives in a stable or a pasture, his home is his castle. It's as much a comfort zone as a herd is. And why not? The stable or pasture is where he gets his food and water and his rest.

Home becomes a magnetic attraction whenever the horse is away from it. You'll find you have to urge a horse away from the barn, but he'll voluntarily pick up the pace when he knows he's heading home. Even when you're riding in a ring, your horse will move faster when he's heading toward the gate, because that's the way back to his stall or pasture.

At no time is this homing-pigeon instinct more evident than on trail rides. When you come to a fork in the trail, you'll find your horse will unerringly choose the path that heads back to the barn. That horses seem to have compasses in their heads is often a good thing. Lost on an unfamiliar trail? Just give your horse his head and let him show you the way home. (Many rental horses also have clocks in their heads; they know when the hour is up, at which point they automatically head back.)

You'll find that confidence—which is an asset in any sport—is especially important in riding. Horses sense human emotions far better than you might think, particularly when a rider emits indecisiveness and, even worse, fear. Horses quickly pick that up and take advantage by bullying or outright refusal to obey the person. School horses are the worst offenders.

What horses don't know instinctually, they learn by *conditioning.* As you'll recall from Psych 101, the word means learning by repetition and reward.

Conditioning is how you teach Fido to sit and "shake hands." You make the dog sit and you say "good dog" and give him a treat. You lift his right paw and you tell him "good dog" and give him another treat. After a while, Fido gets the idea.

Similarly, horses learn to move forward by responding to pressure from the rider's leg. Somewhere in the animal's early education, a trainer on his back relaxed the reins and squeezed his or her lower legs at or just behind the girth. If the horse didn't move, the trainer kept up the pressure and perhaps added a cluck of the tongue or a tap of a whip until forward movement happened. That's when the trainer relaxed the leg pressure; removing the pressure served as the horse's reward. After several repetitions of this, the horse came to understand leg pressure as the signal to move forward.

As well as horses can remember some things, they can't connect making a mistake and receiving a correction unless the correction happens immediately. Anything longer than a few seconds and the connection will be lost forever.

Legendary trainer Gordon Wright observed that "every time you ride a horse, you're either training or untraining him." Consistency is essential. From your very first riding lesson, you'll discover that asking your horse the same way each and every time makes life simpler and more pleasant for both of you.

3

THE WELL-DRESSED RIDER AND HORSE

Certain comic effects can be achieved by a brand-new rider, especially
the man who dresses like a fashion model and rides like a tailor.
—C. J. J. Mullen

Horseback riding is a traditional sport, and nothing demonstrates its ties
with the past more than a rider's formal clothes: boots and breeches,
hacking coats, and hunt caps for English-style riders, or the cowboy
boots, jeans, long-sleeve shirts, and ten-gallon hats for Western riders.

But that's for people who know how to ride. As a novice you'll need
far less in the way of formal clothing, especially until you're sure that
you want to stick with the sport.

FOOTWEAR

Whether you're riding English or Western, the most basic article of
apparel will be your footwear. Sturdy shoes or boots are essential.

"Sturdy" means thick leather footwear that's able to support the foot and ankle (no loafers or low sneakers, please). It also means being able to provide some protection when a horse steps on your foot. Work boots or thick rubber foul-weather boots (the so-called Bean boots) work well, as long as they have heels. Heels are essential, because they keep feet from sliding through the stirrups. That's something you won't want to happen at any time, and especially not if you fall off—being dragged is, well, a drag.

For lessons and informal riding, many English-style riders wear ankle-high paddock boots that lace or zip up the front. There's also an acceptable so-called riding sneaker with pronounced heels.

Tall boots that come to just below the knee support and protect the leg from the knee down. On formal occasions, they're de rigueur for English riders. Field boots look like tall paddock boots, with laces in front of the ankle that make them easier to get into and out of. Dress boots, the style without the laces, look sleeker.

Breeches (pronounced "britches") are worn with tall boots. They're almost exclusively made of sleek stretch fabrics these days.

The idea of buying pair after pair of high boots for growing youngsters may horrify their parents. Help in that regard comes in the form of jodhpur or paddock boots, which are marginally cheaper than high boots. They're worn with jodhpurs, which are breeches that come down to the wearer's ankles.

Here's the good news: As a beginner taking one or two lessons a week, you can certainly get away with wearing heeled shoes as described above and jeans. Tack shops sell clip-on straps that run under the arch of the shoe or boot and keep the pants legs from riding up.

The snugger the jeans fit around your lower leg, the better. However, since constant contact with the horse's sides can cause even the tightest pants to chafe, you might want to consider a pair of leather chaps (pronounced by Western riders as "shaps"). Chaps offer an extra layer of protection as well as support for your leg.

Western riders have it easier, in the sense of having fewer choices. They wear so-called cowboy boots with high heels and pointed toes and jeans with or without chaps.

The very essentials of safety: well-fitting footwear with heels and a helmet with a well-fitted, secure harness.

HEADWEAR

Proper headwear is just as important for horseback riding as it is for bicycle and motorcycle riding, skateboarding, in-line skating, and any other sport in which spills are part of the game. Wearing a hard hat makes excellent sense. Although they're no guarantee against serious head injuries, helmets certainly reduce the chance. That's why most public and private stables now require anyone who rides to wear a protective helmet with a sturdy chin strap. They're also mandatory for most competitive activities, with Western show riding and rodeos as the most notable exceptions.

Helmets come in several varieties. Black or brown velvet hunt caps are traditional for hunter/jumper riding and lower levels of dressage. Brimless "calientes" covered with colorful caps are the kind worn by jockeys and three-day event riders. Helmets with narrow ventilation slits are favored by trail riders and for informal warm-weather riding by many other horsemen.

Whichever you choose, make sure the helmet fits snugly and that the chin harness keeps the headwear securely on your head.

Many lesson barns keep a stack of old helmets available for first-timers or otherwise helmetless riders. Since there may not be one in your size and since the interiors are not always the cleanest (some become mildew farms), you're far better off investing in a helmet of your own.

OTHER APPAREL

With regard to what to wear between your head and your feet, you're pretty much on your own. Many instructors don't like to see their students in thick parkas or floppy shirts, because the clothing masks your posture. A sleek outfit looks better anyway. Cold weather calls for the layered look: a thin goosedown vest over a sweater over a turtleneck or polo shirt. That way you can remove layers as you warm up.

(Speaking of taking clothing off while you're in the saddle, your instructor or someone else should hold your horse's head by the reins whenever you remove a jacket, vest, or sweater. Slipping out of a sleeve or pulling a garment over your head puts you in a very vulnerable position if your horse should decide to shy or even just walk away quickly.)

Gloves are more than an affectation. They keep reins that are wet from rain or sweat from slipping. They also keep your hands warm in winter. Riding gloves are reinforced with rubber or leather along the palms and between the fingers where you'll hold the reins.

Whether to carry a crop (also known as a bat or stick) depends on the horse you're riding. Many school horses will move more willingly in the presence of a crop even if you never use it. Other horses strenuously object to the presence of a stick. Accordingly, your instructor will tell you whether to carry anything.

If you do carry a crop that has a leather loop on the handle, don't put your wrist through it (even though that's what the loop is for). You should learn to switch a stick from one hand to the other in one quick motion, which using the strap won't permit. If you hold a stick in your fist with your thumb on top and the stick resting against your thigh, you won't drop it.

Spurs? Not for novices—not until you develop steady, "educated" lower legs.

Now that you're suitably attired, let's step into the equine department and discuss tack. Although you won't be responsible for outfitting the horse you ride, you should know about what he's wearing and why he's wearing it.

SADDLES
English Saddles

The flat saddle used in English-style riding was developed for jumping. Until just before the 20th century, riders leaned back over fences in the almost supine position seen in old sporting prints. Then an Italian cavalryman named Caprilli had the bright idea of shortening his stirrups. The shorter stirrups closed his hip angle, which allowed him to keep his balance over the horse's center of gravity throughout the jump.

This forward-seat technique, which quickly caught on throughout the military and civilian worlds, required a thinner saddle that gave a closer contact between the horse and the rider's legs and seat than older, heavier saddles did. With only slight modifications, that's the style used today.

You'll most likely ride in what's known as an all-purpose saddle. A widely used choice for general riding, the all-purpose has more padding than the thinner saddles used in dressage and show jumping, and its knee rolls will help keep your legs where they belong.

Saddle pads cushion the horse and absorb sweat. Cotton or synthetics are used. In addition, a foam-rubber pad called a bounce pad is sometimes used beneath the saddle to provide an extra layer of cushioning.

The saddle stays in place by means of a girth that goes under the horse's belly. The girth buckles to billet straps under the saddle flaps.

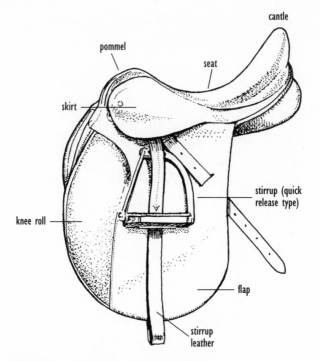

The parts of an English saddle.

Stainless-steel stirrups attach to the saddle by adjustable straps called stirrup leathers. Most stirrups (familiarly called irons) have removable rubber treads that help keep your feet in them. Many beginning riders favor so-called safety stirrups: Instead of a metal fork on the outside, a strong rubber band holds the hinged tread in place. In case of a fall, the rubber band breaks, the stirrup springs open, and the rider's foot isn't caught.

Western Saddles

The Western, or stock, saddle is descended from the seat that medieval armored warriors used. A high front and back (the pommel and cantle, respectively, to be technical) virtually wedged Sir Knight onto his steed and helped keep him there when he was on the receiving end of a well-aimed lance.

The elastic band on a safety stirrup will release in the event the rider falls (photo: author).

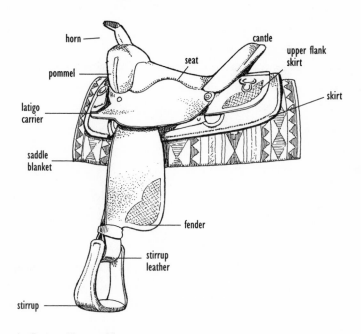

An all-purpose Western saddle.

Cowboys wanted similar security while riding hilly rangeland of the American West or roping cattle. They also wanted a place to tie the end of the lariat; hence, the addition of the saddle horn.

Saddle blankets absorb sweat. Solid colors or traditional Native American designs are popular.

A Western saddle's girth is called the cinch. Some saddles have two cinches, with the one in the rear offering extra security against the impact of roping calves and steers.

Stirrups are usually made of wood and covered with rawhide. The popular Visalia type is bell shaped and has an inch-wide tread. For more secure support, the narrower oxbow shape has a rounded bottom that surrounds the arch of your foot.

Some stirrups are covered by tapadores, or taps, which are hoods that originally protected against thorns or cactus needles. Since they keep a rider's foot from slipping through the stirrup, many riding stables routinely use them on saddles for novice riders.

Note: Like English saddles, Western saddles come in a variety of shapes and sizes to fit both horses and riders. As a novice you needn't be concerned about such matters, since the horses you'll learn on will come equipped with tack. If the seat of the saddle your lesson horse is wearing is too small or too large for you, your instructor will notice the problem and make the necessary substitution.

BITS

Bits fall into three broad categories: snaffle, curb, and hackamore.

Snaffle

Snaffle bits have a level mouthpiece, either one unbroken mouthpiece or two short arms joined in the middle. When you pull on the reins, pressure is applied against the sides of the horse's mouth; the jointed kind also presses against his tongue.

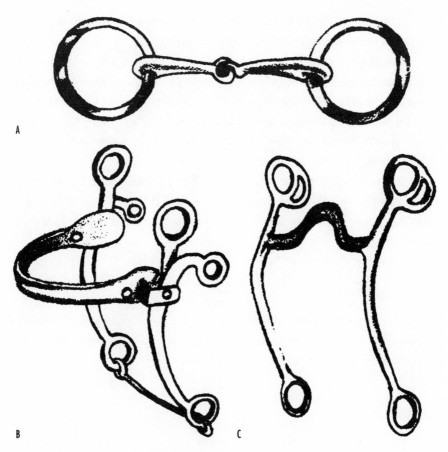

Bits: A. Jointed jointed snaffle (top). B. Hackamore (left). C. Grazing curb (right).

A snaffle is the mildest of bits, and since you'll learn to ride on an agreeable horse that doesn't need much in the way of control, chances are good to excellent that your lesson horse will wear a snaffle.

Curbs

The elevated part of a curb bit's mouthpiece is called the port. The arms to which the reins are attached are called the shanks. The shanks act as levers that move the port against the roof of the horse's mouth; the horse responds to the pressure by slowing or stopping.

A curb becomes more effective when worn with a strap or chain in the so-called curb groove behind the horse's chin. In addition to pressing on that sensitive area, the strap or chain prevents the port from moving too far forward against the roof of the mouth.

A curb bit has far more stopping power than a snaffle bit. That's all that's needed in a bit, because Western horses are taught to neck-rein, or turn when signaled by pressure from a rein against their neck. The usual progression for a Western-trained horse—and rider—is to begin with a snaffle, then move to a curb when the horse's mouth and rider's hands are more educated.

Hackamores

A hackamore isn't really a bit because it's not worn in the horse's mouth. Instead, it fits over the animal's muzzle. Pressure on that sensitive part of the head encourages him to slow down or stop.

Bridles

The bridle is the leather apparatus that holds the bit in place. The crown-piece of an English bridle fits over the head behind the ears and runs down the sides of the head. One end of the cheekpiece buckles to the headstall, the other to one of the bit rings. Another buckle lets you raise or lower the bit for a correct fit.

To keep the bridle from slipping off the horse's head, a throatlatch buckles loosely behind the horse's jowl. The browband goes across the horse's forehead, and a noseband known as the cavesson straps around the muzzle. The noseband can hold a martingale (see p. 27); it also keeps the horse from opening his mouth in a way that reduces the bit's effectiveness.

Western bridles often have only a headstall and cheekpiece. To keep the bridle in place, there's often a throatlatch and sometimes an earpiece that's worn over the horse's right ear.

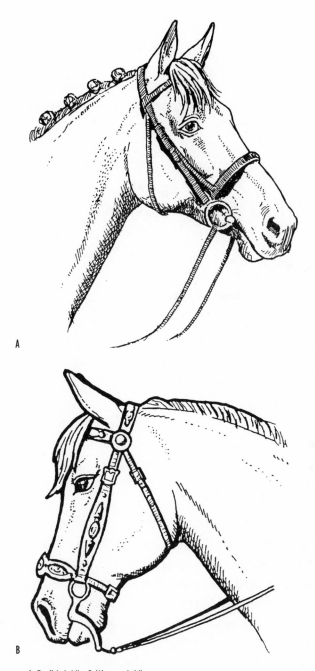

A. English bridle. B. Western bridle

Reins

Reins for an English bridle are two straps buckled at their ends to form a single loop. They come in smooth leather or they can be braided or laced for better grip.

Western reins come in two styles. Texas-style split reins, which are the most prevalent, are a pair of straps that are never tied together. The California style is more complicated. A single closed rein of braided rawhide has a 4-foot strap called the romal, which is attached to a loop or ring at the midpoint of the reins. One of the rider's hands holds the reins just behind the romal, with the other hand holding the trailing piece.

OTHER TACK

Breastcollars and Breastplates

A saddle on a horse with high or low or narrow withers is likely to slip out of position, especially when the horse is climbing a steep hill. That's why many Western horses wear a breastcollar, an apparatus of wide leather straps that go across his chest and withers.

The English-style breastplate has straps on either side of the saddle that meet at the center of the horse's chest. Another strap passes between the horse's forelegs and is attached to the girth.

Martingales and Tie-Downs

A horse that's in the habit of lifting or tossing his head can be literally a real pain, especially if he sticks his nose in the air when you lean forward (human noses have been bloodied or broken after such close encounters). Some horses also raise their heads to evade the action of the bit, which usually leads to a tug-of-war that the horse invariably wins.

Keeping the head down is the job of the standing martingale (English) or tie-down (Western). A leather strap runs from the girth or breastplate ring between the horse's forelegs to the back of the cavesson or, in the case of a Western bridle, to the back of a thin strap around the horse's

A standing martingale keeps a horse from raising his head too high.

muzzle. A standing martingale or tie-down doesn't affect the horse when he's carrying his head normally, but comes into play when he lifts it too high.

The running martingale starts at the girth, goes between the forelegs, and then divides into two straps, each of which fastens to a ring on each rein. It's a more sophisticated piece of tack than a standing or tie-down variety, which is why school horses rarely wear one.

The piece of tack that all horses wear more frequently than any other is the halter. It buckles or snaps around the horse's head and, with the addition of a lead rope or leather-and-chain shank, enables the animal to be easily and securely led or tied.

Like learning the parts of a horse, learning the names of pieces of tack will come in time. Being around horses facilitates the process, and it's a satisfying aspect of becoming an all-around horseman or horsewoman.

But first, since you're probably chomping at the bit to learn to ride, let's meet your horse.

4

MOUNTING AND DISMOUNTING

Never approach a bull from the front,
a horse from the rear, or a fool from any direction.
—Cowboy saying

You show up at the stable for your first lesson. Someone directs you to the riding ring. Standing there is a woman holding a brown horse with a black mane and tail (called a bay). She introduces herself as your instructor and the horse as Fred. The instructor looks pleasant. Fred looks bored. You look expectant. Where do you begin?

Well, since the sport is called horseback riding, you might start by getting up on Fred's back.

MOUNTING

Of the several ways to mount a horse, the easiest is by means of a mounting block. Just about every barn has one or more two- or three-step platforms that horses are led alongside. You climb up the mounting block and swing a leg over the horse's back. Presto!—you're riding.

Okay, using a mounting block is more involved than that—but only slightly. Once you're standing on it, your horse will be led up with his left side next to the block. Always mount a horse on his left side (called the near side). You'll grasp both reins in your left hand, making the right rein slightly shorter than the left one. That way, if the horse moves, he'll swing his hindquarters toward and not away from the mounting block. You'll also hold both reins short enough to prevent him from walking away (although in point of fact, your instructor will hold Fred's head to keep that from happening).

Insert your left foot in the left stirrup, with the tread on the stirrup iron under the sole of your foot. Placing all your weight in that stirrup, put your left hand (still holding the reins) on the horse's neck just in front of the saddle and brace your upper-body weight on that hand.

In one rapid and smooth motion, swing your right leg over Fred's rump. Raise your leg high enough so you don't kick him. Instead of plopping down into the saddle, settle your weight down gently. Horses don't enjoy being plopped upon, and you don't want to start your relationship on a sour note.

Once you're settled in the saddle, pick up your right stirrup. That's the term for inserting your foot. Finding it isn't always easy, but keep probing with your toe. (To save time, your instructor may place your foot in the stirrup for you.)

Another shortcut to mounting is via a leg-up. That's the horsy term for a boost into the saddle. If you been to a racetrack or watched racing on TV, you've seen how it's done—jockeys mount that way.

Stand close to your horse, facing the left side of the saddle. Hold both reins in your left hand, making snug but not tight contact with Fred's mouth to keep him from meandering away.

Balancing on your right leg, bend your left knee so your lower leg juts out behind you at a 90-degree angle. Your instructor or another person will then cup your leg from underneath. At a signal ("1–2–3!" or "*now!*" is traditional), spring up off your right leg and simultaneously

A

B

C

Getting on with the help of a mounting block.

straighten your left leg. You won't need to make much of an effort, because whoever is holding your leg will lift you.

As a result, you'll find yourself soaring upward, high enough to clear
the horse and land in the saddle. Avoid kicking Fred's rump with your right
leg. On your way down, use your right hand to break your fall (no plopping
here either). One caution: Keep your flight on a vertical plane. Too great an
arc and you may find you've gone too far and have overshot your horse.

A

B

Getting a leg-up.

You may have noticed that getting on, whether by means of a mounting block or a leg-up, was done from the left side. Tradition dictates that you mount from that side. You'll dismount that way, too, as well as do many other things to and with horses. Once upon a time in this right-handed world, the majority of men wore their swords on their left hip. Mounting and dismounting from the left side was thus easier, and so the tradition remains. Not that most horses would object if you got on or off from the right side (calf ropers and steer wrestlers routinely do it), but tradition must be served. Another term for the left side of the horse is the *near side*. The right side is called the *off side*.

In other words, the left side is the right side, and the right side is the wrong side.

In this imperfect world there always aren't mounting blocks or people to provide legs-up when you need them. At some point in your riding career you'll have to mount on your own. Here's how:

Stand facing the left side of the saddle as if you were waiting for a leg-up. Hold both reins in your left hand, keeping the right rein a little shorter than the left. That way if the horse moves, he'll swing his hind end toward and not away from you.

Using your right hand to hold the stirrup, insert your foot so the sole is firmly on the bottom. Now brace your left hand on the horse's withers in front of the saddle. Take a pinch of mane in your fingers to avoid leaning on the reins and jabbing Fred in the mouth as you climb aboard.

Reach for and hold the cantle of the saddle with your right hand. In as fluid a motion as you can manage, spring up off the ground with your left foot; as your left leg stands in the stirrup, swing your right leg up and across Fred's back as you did when using the mounting block or getting a leg-up.

However, unlike a leg-up, you're generating all of your own liftoff. You'll need enough energy so your right leg will be able to clear the horse's back; a kick in the rump is as unacceptable as plopping on the animal's back. Actually, it's worse, because Fred might construe the kick as a signal to start moving at a time when that's the last thing in the world you want him to do.

As your right legs descends, sink down gently into the saddle and, once seated, pick up your right stirrup.

A

B

C

Mounting from the ground.

Thanks to the saddle horn, mounting a Western saddle is easier than getting on one of the English variety. Grasp the horn with your left hand and, if need be, use it to pull yourself up as you spring off the ground. If you still have trouble, you can grasp take the horn in both hands, then spring and pull.

Many horses don't stand still during the mounting process, so you should learn to get on as quickly as possible. Dawdling after you insert your left foot in the stirrup opens you to the awkward and dangerous possibility of having to hop on your right foot as Fred walks away.

But, you might ask, what if your horse is too tall? What if you're too short or not limber enough to raise your foot high enough to reach that elusive left stirrup? In that case, feel free to lower the stirrup by unbuckling the leather, dropping it a few holes, and then rebuckling. That should help, but don't make the stirrup so long that your foot swings under the horse's belly as you climb aboard.

Before lengthening the leather, look for sloping ground. With you on the higher side of the hill, you can gain a foot or two or even more. That's often all the advantage you'll need.

A mounting nightmare is a saddle that slips. Make sure the girth is tight enough—you should barely be able to slide your flattened hand between it and the horse's belly (your instructor will show you the proper amount of tension). But since even saddles with tight girths tend to shift, ask anyone standing nearby to help keep the saddle in place. That's done by the person's pulling down on the right stirrup while you mount (in that case, be careful not to kick the Good Samaritan as you swing your right leg over).

But why, you ask, can't the person who's standing nearby give you a leg-up? Answer: Because you need to learn to mount from the ground, that's why.

DISMOUNTING

Much as the idea of spending the rest of your life on horseback might appeal to you, at some point you'll have to get off. You'll be happy to learn that dismounting is a far less strenuous chore than mounting from the ground or even getting a leg-up. Here's how to do it:

Put both reins in your left hand, again keeping them short enough to keep Fred in place. Slide your right foot out of the stirrup. Brace your left hand on the horse's neck in front of the withers (or on the horn of a Western saddle). Placing all your lower-body weight on your left stirrup, swing your right leg over the horse's rump, again avoiding kicking him in the process. As your body moves over to the horse's left side, grasp the cantle of the saddle with your right hand.

You'll end up standing in the left stirrup with your right foot next to your left foot and with your upper-body weight supported by both hands. Now quickly kick your left foot out of the stirrup and slide down to the ground.

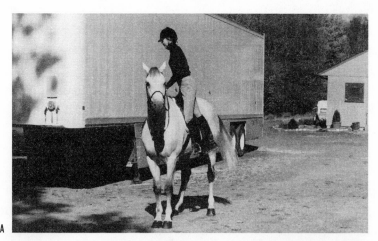

A

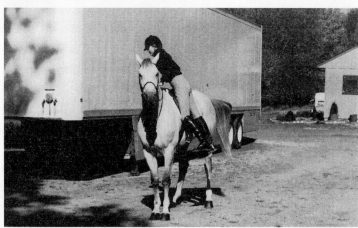

B

Dismounting.

The most important step in the dismounting process is to be sure both feet are out of the stirrups before you slide to the ground. Experienced Western riders can step down off their horses, but the danger of getting hung up is a very real one for novices and for English riders at all levels of proficiency.

Some agile riders like to vault out of the saddle. They put the reins in their left hand, brace that hand on the horse's neck or saddle horn, and kick both feet out of the stirrups. With both hands on the horse's neck or saddle horn, they swing their legs forward to build up momentum, then swing them back in what gymnasts call a scissors-kick. They twist their bodies in the air to get their right leg across the horse's rump. Allez-oop, they land on the ground and on their feet.

Such flying dismounts look flashy, but don't even think about trying them until you're much farther along in your equestrian education—if ever.

Some novices feel that once they're on the ground, they can let go of the reins. Please don't—your responsibility is to hold on to your horse until someone takes him from you.

INVOLUNTARY DISMOUNTS

Skiiers fall, and not just when they're learning to ski. Bicycle riders and in-line skaters fall, too. So do horseback riders. Here's an Equestrian Fact of Life: At some time in your riding experience, you will part company from your horse. The horse may trip or stumble or spook at something, and you'll lose your balance. And the next thing you know you'll be taking a soil sample.

Falling won't make you a member of a very exclusive fraternity, because like manure, "involuntary dismounts" happen. They happen to everyone regardless of whether they're just starting out or have an Olympic medal or two in their trophy case.

A Mexican proverb would have us believe, "It is not enough for a man to know how to ride; he must know how to fall." However, it's been my observation—based on years of research—that most falls happen so quickly you don't have time to prepare. One minute there's a horse between you and the ground, the next there isn't.

Nevertheless, three pieces of advice about falling are in order.

Let go of the reins. There's no way you can restrain a 1,500-pound creature while you're lying on the ground. If you're in a riding ring, the horse will probably just stand quietly; otherwise he might trot over to a friend (school horses have seen more falls than are worth becoming excited over). Even if you're out on a trail far from the stable and you're concerned that your horse will gallop home without you, the injury to your pride will be less painful than a dislocated shoulder.

Don't try to break your fall by using your hands. You're more likely to break an arm. Instead, if you have the presence of mind to do so, try to tuck your chin against your chest and cross your arms across your chest. Again, the operative word is *try* because falls happen so fast . . . even when they seem to happen in slow motion.

If you fall off because your horse stumbled and fell, *try to roll out of his way.* Although a horse will make every effort to avoid stepping on people, his instinct is to scramble to his feet—and you don't want to be too close to his hooves when he does. And if the horse should happen to roll, you'll want to be as far away from him as possible.

Very few falls result in serious injuries. Therefore, when you and Fred part company, just get up, brush yourself off, shrug it off, and climb back on.

OTHER SAFETY TIPS

When you're finished your lesson, you may be asked to take Fred back to his barn. In that case, you'll need to know how to lead a horse.

Like mounting and dismounting, leading is done from the horse's left side. First lift the reins over Fred's head. Your right hand then grasps both reins about 2 feet from his chin The other end of the rein loop belongs in your left hand. That hand can also hold a coil or two of the reins to keep them from dragging on the ground.

To start walking, give Fred's head a couple of short tugs with your right hand. He's more than likely to follow, especially since he knows he's going home. If he doesn't, make two or three click-clucking sounds of encouragement with your tongue.

Just as with the side on which riders mount and dismount, horses are led from the left, or near, side.

Trying to lead a horse by facing him isn't a good idea. First, you'd be walking backward and unable to see where you're going. Second, horses don't like people to stare them in the face while they're walking; they exhibit their dislike by standing stock still.

At the heart (or the sole—pun intended) of the process is keeping your feet out from under Fred's. Walk too close to him and that's just what will happen.

When you and Fred reach his barn, there should be a person there to take him from you. (If for any reason there isn't, wait with him until someone appears or lead him around until you find someone.) The point is not to leave him by himself. "Sit—stay!" isn't a command that equines take to heart.

Nor should you try to put him in his stall without someone there to supervise your putting his halter on him.

Which leads to: It doesn't matter how many times movie cowboys tied their horses by their reins—under no circumstances should you ever do so. When a horse pulls back on reins that are wrapped around hitching posts or stall hooks, the bit will tear his mouth. That's why halters were invented, and that's why they should always be used.

5

BASIC RIDER POSITION

The right way to do almost anything with horses is mainly a matter
of using your natural intelligence in an uncomplicated manner, and
this holds true also for the rider's basic mounted position.
—George H. Morris, *Hunter Seat Equitation*

You've gotten up on Fred via a mounting block or a leg-up or even on
your own from the ground. Your instructor has adjusted your stirrups so
that the bottoms of the irons more or less hit your anklebones. Now let's
put your body where it will have the greatest security and work most ef-
fectively.

Any description of the correct rider position in the saddle begins
from the bottom up. That's because your legs are in a very real sense your
base of support. That anchor starts with the lowest point, your heels.

The single most essential piece of equestrian advice you'll ever receive is simply this: "Keep your heels down." That's the one most common—and heartfelt—suggestion (often, correction) from instructors the
world over.

Simply let your lower-body weight sink into your heels. Instead of making it happen, you *let* it happen (a distinction you'll hear in other contexts throughout your equestrian education).

That's because forcing your weight into your heels is counterproductive. The harder you force, the tenser your ankles become. And tense and rigid joints can't act as the shock absorbers they're intended to be.

You can't keep your heels down unless the stirrup is on the ball of your foot, resting right behind your little toe. Any farther back places the stirrup under your arch, which encourages your ankle to lock. Any farther forward toward your toes, and your foot will slip out of the stirrup.

The outside of your foot, the side your little toe is on, should almost touch the outside fork of the stirrup.

First-time riders tend to turn their toes out as if doing a Charlie Chaplin duck-walk impression. As a result, they grip with the backs of their calves. That tenses the muscles and renders the legs useless as signaling devices to the horse (more on that in the next chapter). Instead, your toes should point out at about a 45-degree angle.

Your calves rest lightly against the horse's side just behind the girth. Think of them as exerting no more pressure than a pair of damp dishrags.

Like your calves, your knees rest against the horse (actually, against the saddle). They don't grip, because gripping would squeeze yourself out of the saddle. Knees that are rigid also can't act as shock absorbers.

Sit in the deepest part of the saddle and on the front of your seatbones, with pelvis pointed slightly forward. Sitting back with pelvis tucked under you, as if in a desk chair, prevents your upper body from moving in sync with the horse's motion.

The rodeo expression (as promulgated by, among others, country singer Garth Brooks) *keep a leg on either side and your mind in the middle* makes as much sense in the riding ring as it does in the rodeo arena. More than that, you want your weight evenly distributed on both seatbones so you're balanced, not leaning to one side or the other. Because your seat is one of the aids, or cues, by which you communicate with your horse, one seatbone pressing harder than the other is giving a signal you don't intend to give. By the same token, a hip that collapses puts

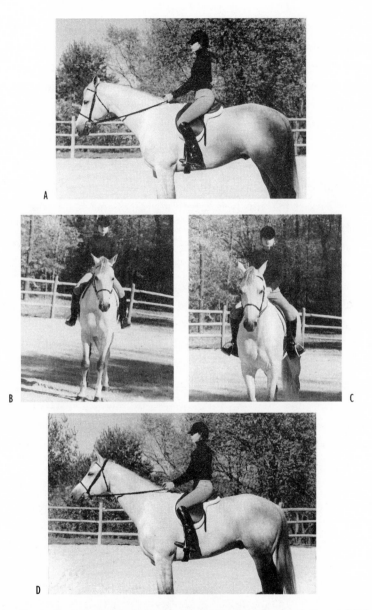

A. A good position on a horse: the rider's head, hip and heel connect in a vertical line. There is also a straight line from her elbow to the horse's mouth. B. The lower leg rests against the horse's side just behind the girth, toes out at approximately a 30° angle. C. Here the toes are out too far, which causes the rider to grip with the back of her leg. D. The stirrup belongs on the ball of the foot, not farther back as shown here.

more weight on that leg, and leg pressure is a primary aid or cue that you don't apply unless and until there's a reason to.

Another Western expression is *sitting tall in the saddle.* That accurately describes how you should hold your upper body. However, "tall" doesn't mean ramrod stiff. Standing at attention may be correct military posture, but a braced back and rigid shoulders and neck will make you tense, and you'll bounce like a sack of potatoes.

Your arms rest comfortably at your sides with your elbows bent. The amount of bend depends on the relative size of you and your horse (see below), but the aim is to create a straight line from your elbow to your horse's mouth.

English-style riders hold each rein between the ring and the little finger, with the bight (the loop end of the rein) held between the thumb and the large knuckle of the index finger. In short, you hold the reins in your fists, with your thumbs up and pointed toward each other so your wrists meet at a 45-degree angle.

Some Western riders hold their reins this way. More, however, hold both reins in one hand in a pincerlike grip formed by the thumb and index finger's big knuckle. The rear portion of the reins comes out of the fist draped over the little finger, as if you were shaking hands with the reins.

The correct way to hold the reins, with thumbs meeting at an approximately 45° angle.

Flat wrists held with the knuckles up drastically reduces the amount of strength and mobility that a rider's arms need.

Hold the reins securely, but not in a tight death-grip fist. Imagine you're holding a damp sponge just firmly enough to keep from dropping it, but not tight enough to produce any water. An alternative image is to hold a bird in each fist just firmly enough to keep it from flying away but without crushing the little fellow.

Elbows that are held away from the rider's sides will restrict the ability to follow the horse's head. They also distract the horse, who can see them out of the corner of his eyes.

Bracing your back so that it's rigid does little to improve your posture in a functional way; it keeps you from moving with the horse's motion.

As for the rest of you, keep your head up and your eyes looking ahead. As you'll discover when you start riding, dropping your head to look down throws your entire upper body out of alignment. Actually, you can discover that fact even before getting on a horse. Look down now . . . as you drop your head, your neck and shoulders drop, too. Even a slight lean changes your center of balance, which a horse will sense and react to.

That's the theory and those are the details. What's even more important is how the parts come together to become an integrated whole.

A horse's "gas pedal," the pressure point where he has been trained to respond by moving forward, is slightly behind the girth (or cinch). To make sure your lower legs are there, try this experiment: Stand straight up in the stirrups (someone should hold Fred's reins so he doesn't walk off). If you feel yourself falling forward toward the horse's neck, your

A rounded, or roached, back deprives your upper body of its strength and looks as sloppy as it is ineffective.

Bracing your legs ahead of the girth pushes your seat to the back of the saddle where you'll bounce around. Moreover, the lack of contact between your lower legs and the horse's sides just behind the girth will deprive you of a primary communication aid.

legs are too far back. Your upper body falling backward means your legs are too far forward. But if you can stand straight up, however unsteadily, your legs are where they belong.

When you're able to stand that way, slowly sink back down in the middle of the saddle. Keep your legs where they were when you stood

Pivoting on your knee forces your heels up and pitches your upper body forward.

up. You should be sitting (remember, on the front of your seatbones) about midway between the pommel and the cantle.

Another way to tell whether your feet are too far forward is to glance down. You shouldn't be able to see your toes. If you can, draw your leg back until your toes disappear just behind your knee.

And keep your heels down, please.

How do you become aware of where your body parts are (or should be)? Although that's one reason why riding instructors were put on this earth, you should take responsibility, too. By training yourself to become aware of the "building blocks" of position—such as whether your heels are down, your hands are at the correct level, and your eyes are looking straight ahead and not down into Fred's neck—you will establish a self-monitoring apparatus that you'll use as long as you ride. And there's no better time to begin than at the beginning of your riding career.

Not everyone has picture-perfect posture on or off a horse. Many of us slouch. To correct this fault on horseback, raise your chest and then

Seen from the rear, the rider's body is centered over her horse.

Here she has more weight on her right hip. The additional pressure of the rider's seat bone and leg will drive the horse to the left, as well as throw off the rider's own sense of balance.

use your abdominal muscles to support your upper body. As suggested earlier, a rigid upper body is wrong. Raising it and then supporting it with your abdominal muscles is correct.

Perhaps your build and Fred's conformation are somewhat incompatible, to the extent that you can't keep your lower legs against his sides without your knees coming off the saddle. Contact by your lower legs is more important than knee contact. That's because your lower legs signal the horse to move, and without such contact you're deprived of your primary communication tool. And that's why you'll be excused if your knees come off the saddle a little bit.

In the best of all worlds, there should be that straight line between your elbow and your horse's mouth. However, a tall rider on a small horse would have to carry his or her hands too low for that, while a short rider on a big horse would carry them too high. In general, your hands will be too low if they graze or touch your thighs or too high if they're above breast high.

There's a very practical reason for keeping a bend in your elbows. You can demonstrate that for yourself with the help of your instructor or another person. With someone holding a rein in each hand just above the horse's bit, straighten your arms and resist against the pressure of your helper's steadily pulling against your hands. You'll find that you have little or no strength to resist and you fall forward.

Now bend your elbows and resist. You can do it now, can't you? That's the kind of advantage you'll need if and when your horse becomes headstrong. Another problem with straight arms is they throw your body weight back, which in turn throws you off balance.

By the way, did I suggest you keep your heels down?

6

OPENING THE GAITS: THE WALK AND THE TROT

Riding is a partnership. The horse lends you his strength, speed
and grace. . . . For your part you give him your guidance,
intelligence and understanding.
—Lucy Rees, *The Horse's Mind*

The signal (or command) that a rider gives to a horse is called an *aid* if
you're an English rider, or a *cue* if you're of the Western persuasion.
We'll use the English term for simplicity.

Although the halt may be every school horse's favorite gait, you'll
want to do more than stand as still as a British Household Cavalry officer
on sentry duty. Okay, let's get moving, starting at the walk.

THE WALK

Even before giving your horse that aid or cue, you'll want the correct rein
length. If there's any loop or droop, tighten the reins until you establish a

light feel of Fred's mouth. The correct way to shorten the reins is to put them in your left hand and slide your right hand up the right rein until you feel a slight contact with Fred's mouth. Then transfer both reins to your right hand and slide your left hand up that rein until there's the same amount of contact.

Many horses interpret the feel of reins being shortened as a signal to move forward. If Fred starts walking after you've shorted the reins, tighten your hands on them as if you're squeezing water out of sponges. That should be all the pressure he'll need to come back to a halt. If the squeezing doesn't work, gradually and gently pull back with your elbows until he stops.

The aid to ask a horse move forward is to close your calves gently against his sides. At the same time, relax your arms so the reins are not restraining him. Feeling your leg aid, Fred may shuffle forward or he may step more purposefully, but he's walking.

Or perhaps he isn't. As noted earlier, the halt is the favorite gait of most lesson horses, so encouraging Fred to walk may take a little more effort. If a few ounces of calf pressure won't work, press a little harder against his sides. Just squeeze with your calves without lifting your legs or raising your heels. In addition, you might try a cluck or two (*cluck* is how riders refer to the sharp vocal clicking sound that conveys encouragement). Again, make sure rein pressure isn't restraining his head.

Still no forward progress? Then increase your lower-leg pressure, perhaps turning your toes out just enough so your heels touch Fred's sides. Add a few more clucks, too, and make them sharper.

The urge to kick a stubborn horse is often overwhelming. If so, restrain that impulse. Sure, a kick or two would get Fred's attention and probably make him move, but at this early stage of your riding career you don't want to sacrifice your correct position in the saddle even for a few moments. That's an easy way to acquire bad habits.

If Fred still hasn't cooperated, you may need to carry a crop. The mere presence of a stick is often enough to motivate some horses. However, since some object to them, your instructor will be the best judge of whether that sort of secondary aid is necessary (sticks and spurs are sec-

A tap with the crop behind the rider's leg will encourage a horse to move forward. Notice that the rider hasn't shifted her position in the saddle, except for the hand that's carrying the stick.

ondary, or artificial, aids that reinforce the rider's legs, hands, seat, and voice).

Don't become discouraged if Fred still doesn't respond as promptly as you'd like. At some point he will, perhaps after a sharp word or a cluck from your instructor; horses often respond to criticism from recognizable authority figures.

Okay, now Fred is walking. The walk has four beats, with the feet hitting the ground individually. The sequence starts with the left hind leg, then the left front (known as the fore), the right hind, and finally the right front.

Your most immediate sensation when you start moving on horseback is swaying. Your hips will swing from side to side, and your pelvis will move front and back. The not-so-secret is to relax and let your hips absorb the movement. Go with the flow.

Let your other shock absorbers—your ankle, knee, shoulder, and elbow joints—go with the flow, too. However, don't relax so much that your heels come up (or your toes drop, which is just as likely); if you do, your legs will swing back far behind the girth.

A good energetic walk with the rider's heels down where they belong.

Make a conscious effort to breathe. Although breathing may seem like the one part of riding at which you're already an expert, lots of people become so entranced by being on a moving horse that they hold their breath. You know from other sports—and from life in general—that you can't stay relaxed without breathing. A relaxed body is a flexible body, so the sooner you become aware of the importance of regular breathing, the more easily you can follow Fred's motion.

MAKING PROGRESS WITH YOUR POSITION

We all start out in our riding careers with a rigid upper body (usually the result of the tenseness that comes with unfamiliarity) and floppy lower legs. However, the correct position is just the opposite: you want secure lower legs that support a flexibly adjustable upper body.

Keep that in mind as you learn to ride, and begin to measure your progress in terms of "quiet" but secure legs and an upper-body control that can maintain your balance as it follows your horse's ever-shifting center of gravity.

Another example of a good walk with the rider's hands following the motion of her horse's head.

A horse moves his head at every walking stride, so your hands must develop a habit of following that forward–backward motion. Actually, it's your arms that follow. As they swing ever so slightly, think to follow more with your forearms than with your elbows or wrists.

It's not an easy thing to learn, especially if your horse doesn't move his head very much (some horses do, some don't). Jane Savoie, a well-known dressage rider and writer, suggests an image you might find helpful: The contact of the horse's mouth through the reins is the same thing you'd feel if you held a piece of wood in a gently flowing stream, as if the pulsating flow of water would pull the wood out of your hands unless your hands gently resist.

If Fred is a member in good standing of the School Horse Union, he'll seize on every opportunity to stop. That's why your legs must remain against his sides—"at the girth," as the expression goes. Don't squeeze if he keeps walking, though—the reward for his listening to your legs is your withdrawing the aid. Otherwise, you'd be nagging. However, if and when you do feel Fred slowing down, increase your calf pressure. Think of your calves as gas pedals: When your car slows down, you press harder on the accelerator to keep it moving.

THE HALT

You've found out how to use the gas; now it's time to learn how to apply the brake, known in horsy circles as the halt.

We've all seen movies in which horses skid to a stop when their riders jerk hard on the reins. Although that qualifies as halting, it's not the educated stop we want. Our goal is a gradual and balanced downward transition. "Balanced" means that the horse will stand with his weight equally distributed on all four legs and his back feet directly behind his front feet.

Remember that a horse is a rear-engine vehicle. Just as your legs got Fred to move forward by activating his hindquarters (his rump and hind legs), so the concept of halting a horse involves keeping him going forward until he reaches your resisting hands.

Making the walk-to-halt transition in that fashion is known as driving Fred up into the bit. As he continues to walk, apply your legs subtly to the spot behind the girth while you squeeze those imaginary sponges in your hands and keep them squeezed with a firm (but not rigid) tension. Even that small amount of pressure on his mouth will encourage Fred to halt. And because your leg pressure drove him up into the bit, he halted in a straight and balanced line.

The alternative of using just the reins would shift Fred's weight to his forehand; he'd plop to a stop as though all the air suddenly went out of him instead of coasting to the smooth and gradual halt you want him to do. You'd find that uncomfortable, too; you'd be jerked forward as if you were a passenger in a car when the driver slammed on the brakes.

TURNING

As you practice your gas-and-brake start–stop transitions between the halt and the walk, you'll reach a point where the riding ring will run out of straightaway. That's where knowing how to turn comes in handy.

Fred is more than capable of staying on the well-trodden path around the perimeter of the ring (known as the rail) and turning whenever the ring curves. But that's not teaching you very much: Keeping a horse balanced and bent smoothly through his turns is an important riding skill.

(By "bent," I mean making a smooth arc from his poll all the way back to his tail.)

Turning a horse may seem like simplicity itself. Want to go left?—pull on the left rein. Going right?—pull on the right rein. However, using both hands creates a smoother turn. One hand initiates the turn while the other keeps the horse bent smoothly.

Let's say you want to go to the left. Start the turn by drawing your left elbow and forearm back, turning Fred's head just to see his left eye. At the same time, let your right elbow and forearm come forward an equivalent distance. The concept is much like the way a bicycle's handlebars work: When one side comes back, the other side goes forward.

While your hands are initiating the turn, your legs maintain Fred's forward momentum. Any pressure on his mouth will encourage him to stop, so use your calf pressure to keep him moving ahead. Maintain the impulsion with your right, or outside* leg, moving it a few inches farther back behind the girth and squeezing a bit harder than with your left, or inside, leg.

Look where you're going. Eye control is fundamental, because looking where you're going helps you turn the horse. Here, as you look left, you'll find that you turn your shoulders to the left, which then turns your hips to the left. Fred will feel that shift in your position and respond accordingly.

When you finish the turn and reach the long side of the ring, bring your right elbow back and your left elbow forward until the reins are even once again. A check point is that your thumbs are even with each other. Move your outside heel forward so your legs are even again, too.

A more ambitious turn is a circle. Halfway down the long side of the ring, turn Fred in off the rail and continue in a loop until you get back to that starting place. The trick to making a circle is to make it as round as possible. That starts with your eyes: Establish an imaginary midpoint around which you'll circumnavigate, then keep your eyes on it (turning

---

*"Outside" means the side away from the inside of the circle. "Inside" means the side closer to the center of the circle. As Fred turns to the left, your right leg is your outside leg, while your left leg is your inside leg.

your head, of course) throughout the turn. Use your hands and legs as you did around the end of the ring, but because Fred is likely to want to tarry in the middle of the ring, you may need to use stronger leg aids.

Speaking of circles, a half circle and half figure eight through the center of the ring are two ways to change direction. Another technique is to make a sharp half turn off the rail, a kind of pivot that will end up with Fred traveling in the opposite direction.

Confusing? Overwhelming? Maybe so, but it won't stay that way forever. At first you'll move the parts of your body only with conscious effort. That's natural. It's how you learned to ride a bike or drive a car or do many other things. Take driving a car, for example. Everything you did the first time you got behind the wheel—accelerating, braking, shifting, steering—required total concentration. The first few times you drove, you hit the gas too hard, you hit the brake too hard or you "rode" it, and you oversteered every turn you made. With experience, however, your driving smoothed out and became second nature, to the point that after a while you drove reflexively. Now you don't need to tell yourself what to do—you just do it. Similarly, the more time you spend in the saddle, often called mileage, the faster your reflexes will take over.

THE TROT

Once you've mastered the walk, halt, and turn, you'll move on to the trot, which is a two-beat gait that's faster than the walk. The horse's feet strike the ground in diagonal pairs: left foreleg and right hind, then right foreleg and left hind.

Moving from the walk into the trot usually requires no more than an increase in calf pressure. You'll easily tell when Fred makes the transition. One minute your hips and pelvis are comfortably swaying back and forth. Then all of a sudden you find yourself bouncing. The feeling is uncomfortable—what's going on here?

You're trotting. And you're right, it *is* uncomfortable. That's why English-style riders learn to post.

Posting the Trot

It's only relatively recently that riders wanted horses that trotted. In the past they far preferred horses that pace, or move their legs on the same side of their body simultaneously (left foreleg and left hind, right fore and right hind). You can see this gait done by Standardbred pacers in harness races or variations done by American Saddlebreds (the slow gait and rack) and by the Paso breeds. Horses that trotted were used primarily for driving coaches and carriages and as cavalry mounts.

Then came the discovery of posting, or rising to the trot. Postillions, the men who control coach horses from horseback (you'll see postillions guiding the horses that pull British state coaches), discovered that raising your seat off a trotting horse's back and then sinking back at the next stride—up-down-up-down—took the sting out of trotting's buffeting effect on the seat of their breeches. As for the name: postillions . . . posting.*

As you walk to the left, watch Fred's outside (right) shoulder move forward and back. When it's moving forward, his right foreleg is on the ground. You want to be rising out of the saddle when that happens, and you then want to lower yourself back into the saddle when that shoulder comes back.

Posting in coordination with a shoulder is called being on a diagonal. When you rise when the right shoulder comes forward, you're on the right diagonal. When you rise when the left shoulder comes forward, you're on the left diagonal.

That is, you post on either the right or the left diagonal, depending on your direction around the ring. If your horse is circling to the left, you belong on the right diagonal. When going the other way, you post on the left diagonal.

(The reason for diagonals, to get technical for a moment, involves the animal's hind legs; specifically, his outside hind leg. Because that leg works harder than the inside hind when the horse is on a circle, the rider's

---

*A historical curiosity: This epiphany occurred during the late 18th century. But since people had been riding for millennia by then, is it not remarkable that the Greeks, Romans, and other "advanced" cultures that made so many other discoveries never came up with posting? What's more, the geniuses never got around to discovering stirrups either.

weight being out of the saddle—that is, the weight not dropping back into the saddle—puts less strain on the outside leg at the moment it's pushing the horse forward.)

Enough theory—now try it. Still at the walk, lean forward from your waist at about a 30-degree angle, while keeping your back flat. As Fred's outside shoulder comes forward, raise up out of the saddle just enough so your fanny clears the saddle. Then sink back down as the shoulder comes back. Don't think of the movement as standing or heaving your body up or plopping down—it's more of a forward-and-backward rocking motion.

Keeping your heels down provides support for your entire body (where have you heard that before?). Your elbows belong at your sides— no flapping. For additional security, grab a pinch of mane in one or both of your index fingers or plant your knuckles on both sides of Fred's crest just below his mane and about a quarter of the way up his neck.

Now get Fred into a slow trot. Glance down at his outside shoulder. Start to post as the shoulder moves forward. Then lower yourself as the shoulder comes back. Up-down, up-down at every stride.

The cardinal sin in learning to post is leaning on the horse's mouth for support. Reins are not water-skiing tow ropes, and your horse won't appreciate your pulling yourself up with them. If and when you feel yourself losing your balance, support yourself with that pinch of mane or your knuckles on Fred's neck. Some instructors buckle a spare stirrup leather around a lesson horse's neck so their students will have something other than their horse's mouth to grab or hold. Yours may do that, too.

To make sure you're on the correct diagonal, glance down at Fred's shoulder. Staring or—even worse—leaning down to look will throw your upper body out of balance. If you're wrong, simply bouncing once (and only once) fixes the problem.

Another method of picking up the correct diagonal is by means of the horse's side-to-side movement. You'll notice your seat swaying as you sit at the trot. When the sway "tosses" your seat to the inside of the ring, let that movement "throw" you up into a post. Then continue the up-down-up-down movement at each stride.

As a practical matter, many instructors don't introduce diagonals until the student gets the hang of posting. But once the subject is raised, being on the correct diagonal ultimately becomes your responsibility. The instructor's "um, wrong diagonal" will over time become a sarcastic "real nice diagonal!" or an exasperated "a-hem!"

After you've trotted to the left for a while, your instructor may ask you to change direction. The easiest way is to trot through the center of the ring and make half a figure eight so you're moving to the right. Changing direction means you'll have to change your diagonal, too. That's simplicity itself: Again, just bounce once. That's all . . . sit out one beat. Up-down-up-down-*down*-up-down-up-down. Glance down, and you'll see you've switched.

The good news is that Fred's increased momentum at the trot makes posting easier than it is at the walk. Nevertheless, posting takes a while to catch on to. You'll bounce and wiggle and wobble and swing and sway and wonder whether you'll ever learn. But everyone else has, and you will, too.

To make the transition from the trot down to the walk, stop posting and open your hip angle so your upper body returns to the vertical. Then, as you did from the walk to the halt, drive Fred up into your re-

Posting the trot with the rider on the correct diagonal: Her body rises and falls at the same time that the horse's outside foreleg and inside hind leg rise and fall.

Posting on the incorrect or "wrong" diagonal: The rider's body rides and falls in time with the horse's inside foreleg and outside hind leg.

straining hands. Fred may take advantage of the situation to "collapse" into the walk as though someone slammed on the brakes. That's why you need to keep his impulsion going with your leg aid throughout the transition.

Don't expect to do everything found in this chapter during your first lesson or even your first two or three. Instructors have their own agendas, and people learn at different rates. Moreover, your first few lessons may last for no more than a half hour each. Riding uses muscles that other sports don't engage, and less is more when it comes to reducing discomfort and increasing stamina.

Thanking your instructor and putting your horse away is the customary way to conclude a lesson. The latter often involves no more than riding or leading him back to his barn and turning him over to a groom. But if you do have the chance to help untack your horse or help bathe him on a hot day, don't pass up that opportunity. The more time you spend around horses, especially in hands-on situations, the more you'll learn about equine behavior and individual personalities.

If he could talk, Fred would add that giving your horse a treat at the end of a lesson is also customary. A carrot or two or one or more lumps of sugar (an acquired taste, so don't be surprised if your horse turns up his nose at the cubes) will suffice quite nicely.

But because horses have terrible table manners and very sharp teeth, be careful how you offer that treat. Hand-feed carefully: palm fully outstretched, with fingers bent back. Better yet, deposit the goodies in Fred's feed bin. He'll be just as grateful.

CARING FOR YOUR MUSCLES

If your muscles don't start complaining a few hours after your first lesson, you'll certainly hear from them by the next day.

A hot bath or sauna helps. So does aspirin or another painkiller. Rubbing alcohol is good and, if you're not averse to the juice of the grain or the grape, alcohol applied within is equally efficacious.

Stretching your muscles before and after lessons is a particularly useful bit of preventive medicine. One exercise starts with standing with your feet wide apart. Bend your right knee about 45 degrees to the right while straightening your left leg. You'll feel the adductor "jockey" muscle—which runs along the inside of your left leg—stretch. Hold that position for 30 seconds. Then reverse: left knee bent and right leg stretched to give your right adductor muscle equal time.

Stretching your hamstrings requires a flight of stairs or a single step. Facing upstairs, stand with only the balls on your feet on one step; your arches and heels should extend out into space. Slowly let your weight sink into your heels. Don't force them down—let them sink. Hold that position for 30 seconds. Repeat frequently.

Another hamstring stretcher is a variation on the jockey-muscle exercise. Stand facing a wall with your feet apart. Place your left foot far enough back from the wall so that you can bend your knee. Your right foot should be almost straight out behind you when you bend your left knee. Lean forward, pressing your palms against the wall. Gently stretch your right foot until it feels as though your heel is about to come off the floor. You'll feel your hamstring stretching. Hold that position for 30 seconds. Then switch legs.

7

MORE TROTTING (AND SOME THEORY)

Forward, calm and straight.
—General Alexis L'Hotte

THE SITTING TROT

As uncomfortable as sitting to the trot may feel, it's the most useful exercise for acquiring a deep, secure seat. And if you're a Western rider, you'll spend lots of time sitting to the slower and more comfortable jog-trot.

Once you've asked Fred for a slow trot, sit erect. Absorb the impact of the trot in your ankles, knees, hips, and lower back. Make especially sure your weight sinks down into your heels and not in your knees. Nor should you try to hold yourself on by gripping with your knees or the backs of your calves—all you'll do is squeeze yourself out of the saddle. Pinch mane or press knuckles on Fred's crest for balance and support—leaning on the reins for security is out of the question.

Doing a sitting trot without stirrups is an effective way to develop a deep, secure seat (photo: Goobertone Photo).

As always, don't forget to breathe. That's especially important at the sitting trot: It's far more concussive than the walk, and breathing helps your body absorb the shock.

If you're *really* adventurous, you can try a sitting trot without stirrups. It's not easy, but it's truly the best way to acquire a deep and independent seat.

Drop your stirrups (that's the term for sliding your feet out of the irons). To keep the stirrup leather buckles from pinching your thighs, pull the front of the leather down about a foot below the stirrup bars. Then crisscross the stirrups across Fred's neck right in front of the saddle.

Once you start trotting, hold your legs and feet just as you would if your feet were in the stirrups: heels down, toes pointed out no more than 45 degrees. Avoid the tendency to drop your toes or grip with the backs of your calves. Sit and breathe and try to follow Fred's motion with your pelvis and lower back.

Trotting without stirrups is hard work. Excruciating, too, especially if your horse decides to pick up the pace (another reason to keep your heels out of his sides). Just a few minutes at a time will be enough. And it's worth it.

THE REIN-BACK

Now that you're on your way to mastering a horse's "forward gears," let's spend a few minutes on "reverse." The term is *rein-back,* which is what the process of making a horse back up is called.

Start with Fred standing at a square and balanced halt. Sit tall and squeeze your lower legs to ask him to move forward. But instead of relaxing and following with your hands as you would as the walk, squeeze the reins and draw your elbows backward.

Those seemingly conflicting aids will make Fred think (and I paraphrase): "The rider's legs are generating impulsion, but I can't go forward because the reins are restraining me. There's no way for me to go but . . . back."

And that's where he should go. If he doesn't, increase the rein pressure and add a cluck until he backs. You'll probably have to repeat the request for each step. The sensation should be that the energy to walk backward is coming from his hindquarters, not from pushing himself backward with his forelegs.

There's no reason to back more than a half-dozen steps. Plan in advance how many you'd like Fred to take. Because of the time lapse between your requests and his responses, relax your legs and hands one step before you want Fred to stop. In other words, if you want five steps of rein-back, relax your aids at the fourth step.

Your legs correct any sideways movement. If you feel Fred's body moving toward the left, push him back with your left leg. Don't raise your heel, but rotate your toe out and press your heel into his side to straighten him. Do the same thing with your right heel if he veers to the right.

Once Fred finishes the rein-back, halt for a beat or two and then make him walk forward. Some horses—and school horses are the prime offenders—back up to evade their rider's aids, so you'll want Fred immediately—and always—to think "forward."

Going around and around the ring will eventually become as boring for Fred as it will for you—probably more if he's a lesson horse that spends his life going around and around rings. To keep him interested and listening to your aids and to practice your skills, you and your instructor can devise exercises that combine the walk, trot, and halt and transitions between them. For example:

- Post the trot along the long sides of the ring, but sit the trot around both ends.
- Post for a dozen strides, then sit-trot a dozen strides. Do another dozen of posting, then a dozen sit-trot. Then go down to the walk for a dozen strides, halt, and rein-back for three steps. Then go to the posting trot through the walk and repeat the exercise. Reverse and repeat.
- At the walk or at the posting or sitting trot, come off the rail at the midpoints of both long sides and circle.
- Serpentines, or slalom turns that cover the length and width of the ring at the posting trot offer the chance to practice both turns and changes of diagonals.

THE IMPULSION PRINCIPLE

A 19th-century French commentator wrote that the three essential responses of a horse are that he goes "forward, calm and straight." At this early stage in your riding career, calm is a given, or else you've been put on a horse you shouldn't be learning on. Straightness is something I'll get to later. That leaves forward.

"Forward" means moving with impulsion. "Impulsion" means energy, in this case energy that's generated from behind. That's because, as is often pointed out, the horse is a rear-engine vehicle. His impulsion, or drive, should come from behind. If not, he'll be pulling himself (and you) along with his front legs instead of pushing himself. That's inefficient and awkward: Imagine that you're a wheelbarrow and Fred is to propel you. He'd be better off pushing than pulling. So it is with impulsion.

Impulsion should never be confused with speed. A horse can walk, trot, or canter at a fast pace without impulsion. He'll feel unbalanced, as if he's running off his feet.

What then does impulsion feel like? In a word, *energetic*. Your horse will feel as though he's driving you forward. The energy that comes from his hind end (horsepeople term it "from his hocks") will make the horse feel springy, with a dynamic and purposeful bounce to his steps.

Another sign that a horse is moving with impulsion is that it feels as though his energy is being transmitted from back to front and as if the energy is shooting out ahead of the animal. That's why your instructor will talk about the need to keep Fred "in front of your leg"—yet another way to describe the sensation that energy is being transmitted forward.

The opposite of "in front of your leg" is, not surprisingly, "behind your leg." That feeling gives the distinct impression that whatever energy the horse has created isn't even enough to get ahead of the saddle. He'll feel blah, like a deflated balloon or a car with a flat tire. Keeping the metaphor of a rear-engine vehicle, this lack of "rpms" will make him less responsive to your aids and, if and when you start jumping or doing another activity that requires energy, you won't have much horse under you.

If you haven't already wondered how you go about creating sufficient impulsion to put a horse in front of your leg, the thought may be crossing your mind right about now.

Creating impulsion comes from a combination of leg and hand aids. Your legs ask the horse for forward momentum by cueing him to generate the rpms from his hindquarters (*engaging his hocks* is yet another illustrative expression). At the same time rein pressure through your hands restrains him. Not so much rein pressure to restrain him to the point of stopping, but enough to keep the energy from escaping . . . think of the energy being bottled up or packaged. And in a very real sense, you *are* packaging that energy by keeping it within your horse.

Done properly, this coordination of leg and hand aids is very subtle and far too advanced for beginners. You won't be expected to master—or even try—it until sometime later in your riding career. Nevertheless, the concept of impulsion is so basic and so important that it's worth knowing about from Day One.

Not all horses have the physical capacity or training to give the response without a great deal of effort on both his part and yours, but you'll know the feeling when it happens. I recall the lesson when my instructor saw how my horse was shuffling along. "Package him," I was told, and then told how to do it. When the horse didn't respond to the instructor's satisfaction, he got on and tried it himself. The effort it took to achieve anything close to what the instructor wanted was painfully obvious.

At my very next lesson I was put on another and far better-schooled horse that responded to my leg and hand aids with no hesitation. The "package" I created felt as though the horse grew another hand or two in height as his body became more compact. The energy generated by his hind end made his steps springier and his forehand lighter. It gave me the sensation that he was indeed in front of my leg. The eye-opening experience set an indelible standard for future riding.

STRAIGHTNESS

Very few horses move in a straight line—their bodies staying straight from poll to tail and their hind feet tracking in the same direction as their forefeet—without help from their riders. Much of this crookedness is far too subtle for novice riders to notice, so at this stage you should be concerned only if and when Fred drifts off the rail or, when you're moving on the diagonal through the center of the ring, he veers from the track you want him to take.

Learning how to keep a horse straight is yet another skill that is best acquired as early in your riding career as possible. It's accomplished basically by pushing the horse back over with your lower leg. If he drifts to the left, you turn your left toe out a few degrees and push your heel against his side at the girth. A right drift is similarly corrected with your right leg. Don't push with all your strength: A firm pulsating push at each stride is just as effective, and your body won't be thrown out of position.

Beginners have a tendency to raise their feet by bending their legs or pivoting on their knees. That causes your lower leg to press above, and not against, the sensitive spot on the horse's side. Keep your leg long, as if trying to reach down under Fred's belly and push up as well as in.

If Fred doesn't listen to your leg, try a little more heel pressure or reinforce your leg with a tap of the crop. If the pressure of your leg and/or

To Videotape or Not to Videotape?

There's no denying that videotaping can be a powerful teaching and learning tool. Someone tapes your lesson, after which you and your instructor review the film with an eye to your form and control. You can then take the tape home for further study and contemplation.

That's the theory. In practice, watching yourself on tape can be a devastatingly brutal experience. Tape tends to exaggerate mistakes in riders' positions and make them look much worse than they really are. If your leg is only a little ahead of the girth, videotape will make it look as though your toe is practically touching your horse's foreleg. Hands that come up just a little higher than they belong will make you look as though you're conducting a symphony orchestra. As a result, you'll focus on what's wrong and pay no attention to what's right. And you won't be happy.

That's why many instructors allow someone to tape their students' lessons, especially lessons of beginning riders, only if the tapes are viewed in the presence of the instructor. In that way the teacher can help the student see the overall picture and place flaws in perspective. Although there may be a glaring error, so many other things may be correct, or at least appropriate for your level of riding, that viewing the problem won't be so upsetting when your instructor is there to explain and encourage.

Actually, the sight of anyone learning the basics of rider form is never a pretty picture. Everyone bounces and flops when starting out (and just wait till you start cantering!). Accordingly, you might want to hold off on the camera work until you've come to grips with the basic gaits.

Once you're comfortable on horseback, periodic videotaping—again, viewed in the company of your instructor—can point out areas that may need work. This is also useful if and when you start jumping, but remember, problems with your form over fences will be exaggerated on tape, too.

On a personal note, I've been glad when tapes of my riding have been available. Not that I'm exactly poetry in motion to watch—far from it—but seeing tapes of horse-show classes immeasurably helps me remember what happened.

That's because my mind tends to go on autopilot the minute I set foot in the show ring. Without a videotape to watch afterward, I'd never remember a thing.

stick encourages him to speed up—after all, that's also the cue for forward momentum—squeeze with your hands and keep him at the pace of *your* choice while you press him over.

This procedure by which a horse moves laterally away your leg is called leg-yielding. It can and should be worked into your exercises: For example, while walking or sit-trotting along the long side of the ring, leg-yield Fred several steps off the rail (moving to the right, use your left leg). Then after a few straight strides, leg-yield him back to the rail. Keep him moving straight ahead, without bending or twisting his forequarters or hind end.

A popular exercise at many barns involves a series of traffic cones set at 15-foot intervals and several steps away from the rail on one of the long sides of the ring. Riders then leg-yield their horses slalomlike around the cones without letting their horses bend their bodies.

You'll discover that leg-yielding works most easily when Fred is moving at a good pace—once again proving that of forward, calm, and straight, forward is the most important.

8

THE CANTER

Be considerate of your horse. He is not a machine—and
even machines run better with good driving.
—Sheila Wall Hundt, *Invitation to Riding*

It's difficult to predict how many lessons will be necessary before you've mastered, or at least come to grips with, the walk and trot (and the halt and rein-back, too). Once you have, however, you'll be ready to tackle the canter.

The canter (or lope, for Western riders) is a three-beat gait. The order in which the horse's legs move depends on whether he's on his right or his left lead. Pronounced to rhyme with "tweed," the word refers to the foreleg that strikes the ground ahead of the other.

A horse that's on his left lead moves with the following sequence of footfalls: first his right hind foot, then simultaneously his left hind and right foreleg, and finally his left foreleg. On his right lead, the order is left hind, simultaneously right hind and left fore, and then right fore.

Preparing to canter: The rider is turning her horse's head toward the rail, which will free his inside shoulder and encourage him to pick up the correct lead.

Being on the correct lead increases a horse's balance and security—he literally has a leg to stand on when going around turns. That's why you'll want to make sure Fred is on his left lead when moving to the left and on his right lead when circling to the right.

Of the several methods to ask for the canter, the easiest is using the outside aids (your outside hand and leg). It's also the method that most school horses are trained in.

Start by cantering on the left lead, which means going to the left, or counterclockwise around the ring. As you walk, shorten your reins until you have a firm—but still a following—contact with Fred's mouth. By using more pressure on the right rein, turn his head toward the rail. At the same time, slide your right heel a few inches farther behind the girth than normal, then squeeze hard with your lower leg.

Turning Fred's head and forequarters frees his inside shoulder, while pressure from your outside lower leg gives him the cue to pick up the canter on the correct (here, the left) lead.

That's the theory. In practice, however, Fred may not be quite so willing to cooperate. Given the reluctance of school horses to work any harder than necessary, Fred may prefer to trot instead of canter. You'll bounce along and squeeze for all you're worth, but even as he keeps his head turned to the rail, he'll continue to trot.

You now have two choices. You can go back to the walk and try again. A tap with a crop behind your outside leg and a sharp cluck or two may make the difference this time.

Or you can cheat. That's basically what running Fred from the trot into the canter is. However, since your goal is to get him to canter, your instructor may prefer this shortcut. (A third choice might be your teacher's getting on and giving Fred a short refresher course in the art of listening to the rider.)

Whichever way you and Fred achieve the canter, you'll know it when it happens. Instead of the "bumpty-bump" of the trot, you'll feel a three-beat "bud-a-*bing,* bud-a-*bing*" rocking-horse rhythm.

Although the canter is a more comfortable gait than the trot, you probably won't think so at first. Depending on your balance (or lack thereof), you may be tossed backward, your butt playing a bongo solo against the saddle. Or you may be tossed forward to the point that you find yourself examining Fred's mane in microscopic detail.

The answer is simply to go with the flow. Keep your heels down— never has this advice been more relevant. Absorb the bouncing with your ankle, knee, and hip joints. Hold your body at the vertical, leaning neither forward nor backward. Feel the forward-and-backward motion with your seat and crotch, and let your pelvis follow it as if you're on a swing. The canter really does have a rocking-chair feeling, and the sooner you adapt to it, the more comfortable you'll be.

You'll also discover that although the canter is a three-beat rhythm, you'll feel it as four, since the moment of suspension when all of Fred's feet are off the ground produces an additional "beat."

Even as you fall into the rhythm with your body, you'll need to follow Fred's head with your hands. That's not easy at first. Until your body becomes steady, your upper body is likely fall back, and you'll catch Fred in the mouth. Result: He'll break back to the trot. Or you might lean forward, known as "leaning up a horse's neck," which puts additional weight on Fred's forehand. Result: He'll break back to the trot.

The trick is to follow Fred's head in a front-and-back motion. Keep your elbows in at your sides, because a "scrubbing" motion with flapping elbows throws you off balance and distracts your horse.

A well-known school-horse trick is to cut corners of the ring. Doing so at the canter is a favorite maneuver. Even more disconcerting is when they duck into the center of the ring. The solution is to keep your inside leg (your left leg when going counterclockwise) against Fred's side, which will hold him on the track by "pushing" him back to the rail. Again, that's not the easiest thing in the world to do while you're still trying to find your balance at the canter.

Drawing your outside hand away from his neck will also help. Trying to hold Fred out along the rail by strong rein pressure won't work; he'll just interpret the pull as a cue to go back to the trot. Instead, hold your hand out with that "holding the stick in the water" amount of pressure while continuing to follow Fred's mouth with a back-to-front motion.

The most prevalent fault of novice canterers is gripping with their knees and thighs in an effort to achieve security in the saddle. On the contrary, all that gripping does is cause you to pivot on your knees, which is the most precarious position to be in. Your lower legs come off your horse's sides, removing the leg aids that will keep him cantering. Moreover, your legs swing forward and backward, and that throws your entire balance out of whack.

Sitting to the canter: The rider is sitting down and around her horse, and she's absorbing the impact in her heels and hips.

Gripping with the knee, a common tendency among beginners who are seeking security, has the opposite effect: It causes the upper body to pitch forward.

Instead, let your lower-body weight slide down into your heels. Try for as long a leg as possible; sit *around* Fred, not just on him (a good image in connection with other gaits, too). That's how you'll achieve security: through balance instead of strength.

Here the rider is carrying her hands too high; there should be a straight line from her elbows to her horse's mouth.

The real paradox—and dilemma—in learning to canter is that you can't learn unless and until your horse canters, but he won't canter unless and until you ask him correctly and then keep him cantering . . . which you can't do until you learn to canter.

A way around this dilemma is by *longeing,* pronounced with a soft *g* and as if it were spelled "lunging." It's a method of exercise a horse without riding him, by which the horse circles the handler, who controls the animal by means of a long line called a longe line (pronounced "lunge line"). Longeing is also used to train riders; with the handler keeping the horse moving, the reinless rider can concentrate on developing a deep and independent seat. It's a particularly good way to learn to canter, since Fred or another horse that's accustomed to being longed will continue cantering without being jabbed in the mouth (your instructor's voice and a long whip will provide all the encouragement he needs). See whether longeing is available where you ride, and take advantage of it if you can.

By the way, recruits at Vienna's Spanish Riding School—one of the world's preeminent classical dressage establishments—spend their first six months being longed without reins or stirrups.

Cantering without stirrups encourages a deep seat. Keeping your heels down is especially important for security when you ride without stirrups at any gait.

Just as humans are right- or left-handed, so horses prefer one lead or the other, and getting some school horses to take the less favored one can be a herculean labor. If Fred picks up the incorrect lead, your instructor may or may not make an issue out of it. Since the object of the lesson is to acquaint you with the canter, Fred's being on the wrong lead isn't the end of the world if the alternative is a major hassle.

When it's time to make the transition from the canter down to the trot or walk, brace your back for support and use your lower legs to drive your horse into your restraining hands. You've done it to go from the trot to the walk, and the technique is the same here. Simply pulling back on the reins will cause Fred to stop abruptly and awkwardly and put too much of his weight on his forehand. He'll plop to a stop, and you'll fall forward.

The simplest way to change directions is to make the downward transition from the canter through the trot to the walk, turn 180 degrees, and then walk off in the new direction.

Or you can change direction through the center of the ring in a half figure eight. Canter off the rail into the center of the ring, go down to the walk or trot, and turn your horse in the new direction (if you've been cantering counterclockwise, for instance, you'll turn right). To pick up the canter, apply your new outside rein and leg aids. Don't be too concerned if Fred doesn't give you a canter pickup immediately. Just keep at it. The rail, when you reach it, will help keep Fred going in the new direction and will also prevent him from evading your aids.

Another way to change leads is called the flying change. A well-balanced and well-trained horse is able to switch from one lead to the other while maintaining the canter. You ask for the swap primarily with your seat and legs, and the horse responds by shifting his weight and changing leads while his feet are off the ground. (Thoroughbred race-horses do it at the top of the stretch, while high-level dressage horses can change leads every third, every second, and even every stride.)

Getting a flying change requires a rider with a good sense of balance and timing and a horse that's been schooled to respond to the aids. You're not ready for such sophisticated work, and since few school horses have that level of education, neither is Fred. Admire those horses and riders that can do flying changes, and be satisfied with clean and accurate simple changes of lead through the trot.

THE HALF-SEAT

English riders who plan to go on to jumping have an alternative to sitting the canter called the half-seat or two-point. Its purpose is to keep you in balance with your horse's center of gravity as the two of you approach and then jump a fence.

Instead of using both lower legs and your seat (actually, your crotch) in the three-point position that you've worked on so far, you'll raise your seat out of the saddle. The only contact between your body and the horse will be with your lower legs—hence the name *two-point.*

(Interestingly, Jockeys ride in an exaggerated two-point seat, not only to get up over their horses' center of gravity, but also to cut down on wind resistance.)

Try the two-point at the walk. With weight in your heels, incline your waist angle some 30 degrees as if you were posting. But instead of sinking back into the saddle, hold yourself up. Press your hands against Fred's crest to support yourself if you need to.

This two-point position (somewhat exaggerated for visual effect) should be the same upper-body angle as the "up" position in posting.

If you feel yourself falling forward, your legs may have swung back. Go back to your normal three-point position, check to make sure your legs are where they belong, and try the two-point again, this time making sure your lower legs don't slip.

Now ask Fred to trot. Hold that position, keeping your knuckles on his neck for support.

Go back to the walk and your three-point seat to ask Fred to canter. Once he's cantering, however, go up into your half-seat. Keep your butt just high enough to clear the saddle. Keep your legs long and absorb the impact in your heels. You may well find yourself relaxing because, as you'll discover, cantering in a half-seat can be much easier than in a three-point.

As you become adept at sitting to the canter, you should learn to feel which lead your horse is on. Glance down at Fred's shoulders and notice whether his inside shoulder is preceding his outside one. If so, make a note of the feeling, which becomes more pronounced around turns. If the outside shoulder precedes the inside one, he's on the wrong lead. That will give a slightly arrhythmic and unbalanced feeling—note that, too.

Another way to tell you're incorrect is to listen to your instructor. Instructors are as good about shouting "wrong lead!" as they are with "wrong diagonal!" If you're on the wrong lead, go back to the trot and try again.

THE GALLOP

The gallop is something of a fast canter, but little more needs to be said about it here, other than that the gait is rarely used by novice riders in a ring—at least not intentionally. Galloping requires a secure seat and a horse that's willing to go at speed.

I'll discuss galloping in the next chapter, in connection with trail riding.

9

TRAIL RIDING

O the horseman's and horsewoman's joys!
The saddle, the gallop, the pressure upon the seat,
the cool gurgling by the ears and hair.
—Walt Whitman, *Leaves of Grass*

Once you've developed a secure seat at the walk, trot, and canter, you're ready to leave the ring and go trail riding. It's a big step not only in your equestrian progress but also in the way your vistas will expand. Whether you're on a well-manicured bridle path in an urban setting or off the beaten track, seeing your surroundings from the saddle takes you back to nature in an ancient yet enduring way.

Fred will enjoy the change of scenery as much as you will. Even the most placid and seemingly uncaring horse finds fresh energy once he leaves the ring. That's especially true for horses that don't get out much; they become "ring sour," for which the antidote is a change of scenery.

On the other hand, the equine mind views the outside world as a place that's fraught with perilous possibilities. Who knows whether a mountain lion lies in wait around the next corner? Or what danger lurks in a sheet of paper blowing across the trail? Eons-old instincts die hard.

One of the joys of trail riding is the option of finding solitude on horseback (but—for safety's sake—only when you're capable of riding out by yourself).

Therefore, since your horse is likely to be on his toes, you should be, too. Rule Number One of trail riding—and for that matter of riding in general—is to stay alert. Never take anything for granted.

A solitary jaunt may seem like fun, and challenging too, but save that for later. Your first few trips should be in the company of at least one other rider—an experienced one at that—until you and your instructor feel confident about your ability to handle a horse by yourself.

COPING WITH SHYING AND BOLTING

Before you venture forth, plan to spend a few moments learning to deal with unexpected equine reactions you might encounter.

A sudden or unfamiliar sight or sound can attract Fred's attention: a bird flying out of a bush, a startled deer bounding away, or a dog bounding toward him. Nine times out of ten he won't think twice about it. But horses being horses, every now and again even the most bombproof beast will react.

Shying happens fast, much faster than you think possible. One minute Fred is amiably ambling along. A split second later he has propped his front feet, twisted his body, and taken a few quick steps away from whatever object of terror caught his attention.

The momentum of Fred's shying will throw you off balance, and most likely you'll fall forward toward, if not against, his neck. That's not good. Leaning forward is the most vulnerable position for you to be in, because if Fred turns and drops a shoulder, you're on your way to the ground.

Grabbing Fred's neck will be your initial impulse, even though your upper body may be flat against it. Bad idea. Instead, sit up. Sitting up restores your balance and with it your security in the saddle, and it puts you back in a position of control.

Nine out of ten shies last no more than a few seconds. The skittishness is quickly followed by the equine equivalent of a calmer but embarrassed, "Gee, I was certain that sight or sound had to be scarier than it really was." However, what starts as a little skitter can sometimes escalate into full-fledged bolting.

Any discussion of potential problems on the trail would be a good place for a few words on the general subject for rider attitude. Horses, being herd creatures, are genetically programmed to take their cues from others, and that includes the people on their backs. Any apprehension on your part that something terrible might happen will be communicated to your horse by tension from your legs, hands, and seat. The animal's response will be a similar, "Ohmigod, there's something to worry about." Who can blame him?—you obviously know something that he doesn't.

That often happens where I ride. The trails are shared by carriage horses that are driven as singles, pairs, or four-in-hands. The clip-clop of multiple sets of hooves, the scraping of carriage wheels on gravel, and the jingling of harnesses are unfamiliar sounds that attract attention of horses and riders. Although the drivers are sensible about slowing down and waiting, now and again a ridden horse will dance in place or back away from a carriage that gets too close. But instead of adopting a "no-big-deal," reassuring attitude, many riders panic at the prospect of what might happen if their horses bolt. Their horses sense their anxiety and behave even sillier, yet another example of equestrian self-fulfilling prophecies.

Although telling anyone to relax is largely a waste of breath (when was the last time you obeyed the command, "Relax!"?), let me merely suggest that to the extent it's possible, when a potential problem arises make an honest effort to keep your wits about you. Instead of imagining the worst, imagine the best—solving the problem before it happens or, if not, as soon after it happens as you can.

THE PULLEY REIN

Being run away with is no fun at all. The proper response is to stop your horse, but like being told to relax, that's often easier said than done. However, there's a valuable tool for such situations: an "emergency brake" called the pulley rein.

Get acquainted with the pulley rein before you go out on your first trail ride. If you're right-handed, brace your left hand (while holding the rein, of course) on the top of Fred's neck about a foot or two in front of his withers. Put your thumb on the right side of his neck and the rest of your fingers on the left. Push your feet ahead to brace your legs against the stirrups. As you also brace your left hand against Fred's neck, pull directly back with your right arm. The pulley (actually, a lever) action max-

The pulley rein is an "emergency brake:" one hand braces against the horse's neck while the other hand pulls hard on the rein.

imizes your strength. If Fred doesn't stop immediately, he will shortly thereafter.

Another technique, if there happens to be enough open space, is to make gradually decreasing circles, which will "spiral" Fred to a stop.

Chances are you'll never have to deal with a runaway, but knowing how to stop one is a valuable tool in your emergency kit.

RIDING IN GROUPS

Horses can undergo personality changes when they leave the ring. A quiet one can become assertive and prefer to lead the herd, even if the herd consists of just one other horse. Others like to hang back. On the other hand, still others couldn't care less.

It won't take long before Fred's trail personality becomes evident. Which position in the group he should occupy is something he may dictate by forging ahead or lagging behind. Then, too, some horses become upset when they're separated from their buddies. Others may balk, bare their teeth, and lay their ears back as an objection to being close to horses they don't like. But don't worry—the experienced rider who is escorting you can arrange a safe and comfortable order of procession.

Ride in single file, with a minimum distance of one horse length between Fred and the horse in front of him. That spacing prevents crowding and the opportunity—if not an outright invitation—to kick or be kicked.

Ride side by side only when the trail is wide enough, and never more than two abreast. Staying stirrup to stirrup even when you're out with one other rider can be more difficult than it would seem. Horses walk at different speeds, and if Fred is a shuffler when your companion's horse is a pacesetter, you'll find yourself lagging behind.

Stay in line and keep in your place in the cavalcade. If you must pass, do so only when there's enough space on the trail not to crowd the horse in front.

If and when you come to a steep slope, stay two lengths apart going uphill and three lengths when going down hill. That spacing reduces the chance of collisions in case there's any slipping or sliding.

Speaking of ups and downs, lean forward when you're climbing steep hills. Force your weight into your stirrups. Grab a pinch of mane or the saddle horn to keep your balance. Keeping your weight off your horse's hindquarters frees them for their job of pushing up a hill. Since horses use their necks for balance, slide your hands forward to give plenty of rein.

Some horses will canter up steep slopes for better hind-end traction.

Descending a steep slope calls for a different technique. Lean back just far enough to stay in balance. Keeping lots of weight on your heels is even more important here than when going uphill. Maintain a light feel of your horses' mouth, but don't let the reins restrict Fred's head as he works his way down the hill.

Riding one-handed gives you a chance to relax the other hand or, for that matter, scratch an itch or emphasize a point in your conversation. Try it while you're walking along. Separate the reins with your little finger; otherwise, hold the reins as you normally do. You may even find that following Fred's mouth is easier one-handed than it is with two.

Holding a tree branch for the rider behind you is misplaced politeness. Before the other rider is able to grab the branch or brush it aside, it will have snapped back, usually right into that person's face. Plus, your horses will be too close to each other.

However, feel free to hold gates open until everyone else has passed through. Then make sure the gate is closed and fastened.

Most trail riding is done at the walk, especially the first mile or so out to give the horses a chance to warm up. However, stretches of trotting are certainly to be encouraged on reasonably level ground and uphill terrain. Don't be concerned about diagonals, but changing once or twice during long trots is easier on your horse's back and legs.

A canter is great fun over level ground or up a hill. Being on a particular lead doesn't matter on the trail unless you know or are told that a sharp curve lies ahead. If the pace is sedate, you can canter in your three-point position, but when it picks up you may want to get up into your two-point position. It's easier on both you and Fred.

Canters often become exuberant, especially when one horse becomes a little headstrong and the others try to keep up. As the pace increases, Fred will level out his body into a smoother ride for you, and his gait will turn into four beats. That's a *hand gallop,* so called because you have your horse in hand (meaning control). Get up into a two-point contact, and enjoy the sensation of the wind whistling past your ears as your horse below you bounds ahead in ground-eating strides.

Cantering makes sense only if all the riders can handle their horses in a group situation. That's because equine attitudes and instincts about competition and running with the herd can turn what starts out as a moderate lope into the Kentucky Derby. If you find yourself going faster than you want to and Fred doesn't listen to reason, the magic word is a loud "whoa!" to let the rider in the front of the group know that you want to stop. For more stopping power than a steady pull on the reins gives, try "shifting the bit," which means alternating pressure on the reins in a seesawing motion.

And should you need it, there's always the pulley rein.

Girths frequently need tightening after the strain of cantering or going up or down a steep hill. To tell whether there's less tension, put both reins in one hand and then reach down and see whether you can slide your hand under the girth more easily than when you began your ride.

At this point in your riding career you should be able to do the tightening from the saddle. Practice in the ring: Put both reins in your right hand and swing your left foot ahead of the saddle's knee roll. Reach down and unbuckle the rear billet strap (without letting it go, of course), then pull it up to the next hole or two and rebuckle. Then repeat the process with the other billet. It's an easier job than you might think, because your position in the saddle gives you plenty of leverage to pull up.

Before you stop to check or tighten the girth, be sure to alert the other riders to what you're doing. That's so they can halt, too. No horse on the trail likes to stand still while others are moving away from him. In addition, warning any riders behind you that you plan to halt will prevent pile-ups.

No trail is perfectly level. Even the gentlest undulation will have an effect on your horses' balance, which in turn affects your position. That's a real benefit of trail riding: Changing your position, especially your upper body, to compensate for Fred's changes in balance will make you a more sensitive rider. Feel free to experiment with how much you need to open your hip angle and lean back when you're going down even a slight hill. Or close your hip angle and incline your upper body when going up a rise in the road. Nothing in riding is static, especially not out on the trail.

Your ability and stamina will determine the pace, duration, and route of your ride. So will the weather and footing conditions. A very hot day is just as uncomfortable for Fred as it is for you, so walking with a very occasional trot will be the order of the day. Snow may turn your trails into a winter wonderland, but a layer of ice underneath can hide slippery hazards (although horseshoes fitted with borium studs that act as cleats will help). Hard ground in any climate is the equine equivalent of pavement. Trotting and certainly cantering make horses become footsore and possibly lame from the pounding.

In all instances, your horse's owner or your experienced companion will determine when, where and how long to stay out.

TRAIL-RIDING SAFETY AND ETIQUETTE

- Keep one horse length between you and the horse in front. Stay two lengths behind going uphill and three lengths going down a steep hill.
- Ride side by side only when the trail is wide enough. Otherwise, stay one behind the other.
- Give the horse you're passing a wide berth if you must pass. And let the rider(s) in front of you know that you're moving ahead.
- Don't hold branches for the rider behind you, and don't anticipate that the rider in front of you will hold them for you.

Some trails post their "Rules of the Road." (photo: author).

- Make sure everyone has plenty of warning whenever the group will change gaits.
- Don't ride faster than a walk or slow jog-trot around blind corners. Riders or pedestrians may be coming the other way, and they can't see you either.
- Riders who approach each other at different gaits are expected to pass at the slower gait. If you're trotting and the other rider is walking, it's your job to slow down and walk.
- Holes and other hidden hazards await horses that stray off the path. Leaving the trail is also likely to tear up foliage. Similarly, a closely mowed pasture that looks like a turf paradise for riding can have hidden woodchuck or rabbit holes. Moral: Stay where you belong.
- When a trail runs along a paved road, keep off the pavement whenever possible. However, don't get so far away from the road that you end up in ditches or tall grass that can hide holes or discarded glass bottles.
- If riding along a paved road is unavoidable, stay to the right as if you were in a car. And ride in single file.
- Staying in single file is also appropriate when crossing a road. An experienced rider or the group leader will move out of the line to

Access to trails may involve riding along paved streets or roads. Because this road was closed to vehicles, the riders could stay side by side and give a wide berth to a cyclist who didn't keep to the right. (photo: author).

signal any traffic to stop until the other horses are safely on the other side.

- Don't assume that drivers of cars and trucks will automatically slow down when they see horses. The hand signal to request a driver to reduce speed is a palm-down, up-and-down wave, as if you were slowly dribbling a basketball. Then show your gratitude with a nod or a wave.

- Many riding trails, and especially those through parks, must be shared with nonriders. Staying on the right-hand side of the trail will help keep you away from hikers, bike riders, dog walkers, and others. As with drivers, don't take for granted that everyone knows or agrees that horseback riders have the right-of-way. Case in point: Even though the bridle path around New York City's Central Park reservoir is designated as such, joggers and dog walkers routinely crowd the path. Many of them even resent the presence of horses. That's why you should develop the riding reflex of anticipating potentially dangerous situations and then acting accordingly—defensive riding makes as much sense as

Sharing bridle paths with joggers is a common urban experience (photo: author).

So is contending with dogs on leashes (photo: author).

defensive driving does. For example, a baby carriage or a dog that's barking or pulling against a leash can upset a horse. Don't hesitate to ask the carriage pusher or dog walker to move to a wider part of the trail or at least to the far side.

- Unfortunately, no matter how hard you try to anticipate trouble, someone may do something that will cause your horse to spook. If so, calm your animal without becoming flustered yourself. The advantage to being in the company of an experienced rider is readily available good advice about what to do and how to do it.

- Signs that say POSTED LAND put you on notice that you have no right to be there. However, many trails cross private land over which owners have given permission to ride, and they deserve special attention. Make sure gates are securely closed after you've passed through them.

- Don't litter. Nothing alienates landowners faster than finding trash along a trail. However, you'll win points by informing the owner about broken fences, downed trees or power lines, and other items that need attention.

- Finally, just as you gave Fred a chance to warm up by walking the first mile out, let him cool off by walking the last mile back to the barn.

10

OVER THE GATES: BEGINNING JUMPING

The quality of the jump is determined by the
quality of the approach to the fence.
—Mary Wanless, *The Natural Rider*

Although many English-style riders are perfectly content to concentrate on trail riding, dressage, or any of the other earthbound activities, lots of others become smitten with jumping. And for good reason: Few things in horse sports match the thrill and delight of becoming airborne. Even after thousands of years, Pegasus remains a potent symbol.

Taking lessons to learn to ride is useful. Taking lessons to learn to jump is crucial. Although safety should be your primary concern, supervision is more than just a matter of maintaining human and equine life and limb. Problems that involve body position and timing crop up from time to time, and they need to be nipped in the bud. That's why everyone who jumps—from Olympians on down—works with a trainer, someone who can make assessments and corrections from a vantage point on the ground that takes in both horse and rider.

Before visions of you and Fred soaring over formidable Olympic-sized fences dance in your head, let me hasten to advise that jumping such "big sticks" on Fred isn't even an option. School horses have their physical limitations, of which safely jumping anything much higher than 3 feet is one. If after you learn the basics you're eager to move up to more demanding fences and courses, you'll have to move on to another horse. But until then, Fred will do just fine.

BUT FIRST, A BIT OF THEORY

Trail riding up and down hills has already given you something of a feeling for what a horse does with his body over a fence. Taking off at a jump is similar to how a horse goes uphill: He shifts his weight to his hindquarters, which he uses to propel him up and over the fence. His center of gravity then shifts to his forequarters for the landing, this time moving similarly to going downhill.

The job of the rider during the jump is (in theory anyway) to do as little as possible to interfere with the horse. That's easy, because it involves nothing more than staying in balance. But what's easy in principle is difficult in practice, because doing nothing can be hard. Just wait, you'll see.

A basic course of eight fences might take Fred approximately 100 strides from start to finish. Eight fences means only eight extra-long strides (which is all that jumps are) in which *he* does all the work. That leaves 92 normal strides in which you go to work: that is, keeping him balanced and at a steady pace between the jumps and then guiding him to optimum takeoff spots. Compared to all that piloting and navigation, jumping is a piece of cake.

In the best of all worlds a horse jumps in a perfect arc, leaving the ground as far away from the obstacle as it is high and landing an equal distance beyond. The math is simplicity itself: a takeoff 3 feet away from a 3-foot jump and a landing 3 feet beyond.

However, in this imperfect world a horse will sometimes leave the ground too close to the jump. The obvious consequence is hitting the fence with one or both of his forefeet on the way up. Or he may leave too far away from the fence, in which case he's likely to hit the fence with his hind legs on the way down.

Like a track-and-field high jumper looking for the optimum takeoff point, you'll adjust Fred's stride so he leaves from what you consider an acceptable if not perfect spot (also known as the distance). You needn't be a high jumper to understand how to do so. If you can cross a street without tripping over the far curb, you already know how to lengthen or shorten your stride so you don't trip over the curb or have to take a giant last step to reach it. That's the same thing you'll learn to do with Fred: You'll lengthen or shorten his stride to get to that good distance.

But not for a while.

You'll begin your first jumping lesson by warming up on the flat. Make sure all three of Fred's gaits are active. Fred should be "thinking forward" and listening to you.

Making the transition between flat work and jumping starts with shortening your stirrups by one or two holes. The shorter length helps you incline your upper body, which, as you're about to learn, helps keep you in balance with a jumping horse.

A pole on the ground doesn't look like much of a jump, but it is. Your trainer will place several rails (poles that stretch across jumps) around the ring.

You'll start by walking Fred over one of them. Look at something directly beyond the rail—perhaps a panel or a post of the fence that encloses the ring, or a bush or tree on the outside of the arena. Pick something high enough off the ground so that your gaze is level, not downward. Now ride Fred toward that target, steering toward the mid-point of the ground rail.

Eye control is crucial. To see where you are in relation to the rails, drop just your eyes for a split second. If you stare at the rail, you'll drop

When trotting crossrails, keep your eyes up and focused ahead on an object that's on a straight line away from the rails.

your head, which will cause your upper body to tilt. That in turn will put too much weight on Fred's forehand, and he'll slow down.

But if you steer for the center of the rail and keep your eyes up and your legs on Fred's sides, he'll step right over the rail.

Soon you'll be walking over all the rails. Then trotting over them. Trotting involves the same technique. The only difference is the poles come up a little faster than from the walk. Maintain a steady pace, steer for the middle of the rails, and if and when you look at the rails, do so with only a quick downward glance.

If Fred kicks any of the rails, he'll just have to remember to lift his big feet.

Cantering over ground rails calls for more accuracy on Fred's part—and yours. Try to place his front legs as close to the rails as possible without stepping on them. If a few strides away you sense he's getting too close to the rail, shorten Fred's stride by opening your hip angle. That is, draw your shoulders back (keep your legs on his sides and continue to follow with your hands). If that doesn't work, try sitting up and closing your fingers on the reins.

However, if you sense that Fred's front feet will be too far away from the rail, move him up by more leg pressure and slightly less rein pressure. After being warmed up on the flat, Fred should listen to your leg aid. If he doesn't, reinforce the aid with a cluck or two or a tap of the crop behind your leg.

Many beginners who have no trouble walking and trotting over ground rails run into difficulty at the canter. That's because they make a big deal of the poles: "Canter-canter-canter . . . uh-oh!—here's comes the rail . . . here it comes . . . I should be doing something . . . it's *here!*"

That's cantering *to* the rail, not cantering *over* it. Ride to whatever distant object you've fixed your eyes on. You don't focus on the curb when you cross the street; you step over it and continue along your merry way without altering your pace. Treat the ground rail no differently.

An exercise that's very useful in developing a sense of pace and distance is to canter between two ground rails that have been set a predetermined number of strides apart. Two rails 66 feet apart can be ridden in either four strides in a lengthened canter (achieved by your active lower legs) or five strides in a shortened "packaged" canter.*

Alternate between the four and the five strides. Feeling and then committing to "body memory" the difference between a forward pace and a shortened one will be very helpful when you start cantering between jumps.

The amount of time you need to develop the ability to see for distance will depend on your sense of pace and timing. A few blessed souls have a natural feel and never miss a good takeoff spot, while the majority of us mere mortals achieve the skill by plenty of trial and error. That's why we practice . . . and why we have instructors to help us.

---

*The math is based on a horse that canters on a 12-foot stride (Fred's canter step may measure less—your instructor will know).

The landing stride off a fence is one half the horse's normal stride, so subtract 6 feet. The takeoff stride is also half the normal stride, so deduct another 6 feet. That leaves 52 feet. A normal four strides at a 12-foot step would measure 60 feet ($4 \times 12' + 6' + 6'$). A normal five strides would measure 72 feet ($5 \times 12' + 6' + 6'$). Sixty-six feet is halfway between, so it can be ridden either in four long strides or five shorter ones.

Some barns and instructors use cavaletti, which are rails that can be adjusted to heights between the ground to about 1½ feet off the ground. These are introduced after you master ground rails, and their additional height is enough to encourage Fred to lift his feet and give more of the sensation of jumping.

More likely than not, your first real fence will be a low *X*, or cross-rail, no higher than 18 inches at the spot where the two rails intersect. Your instructor will also place a ground rail a foot or two in front to give Fred visual assistance in judging his takeoff spot.

A good jump begins with a good approach. Give yourself plenty of time and distance—perhaps halfway around the ring—to establish an active trot. You'll want Fred in front of your leg with impulsion but not speed. Anything too fast will unbalance Fred, while a trot that's too slow won't have the necessary energy to produce a good jump (he'd have to heave himself over the cross-rail in sections, like a caterpillar).

Six or so strides from the fence, you'll stop posting. You'll rise into a two-point position: upper body inclined approximately 30 degrees, your butt just out of the saddle, and your weight well down into your heels. It's much the same position—and feeling—as when riding up a steep hill on the trail.

You'll also slide your hands approximately halfway up the sides of Fred's neck. Support your upper body with the bottoms of your fists, with your thumbs touching his mane. Allow enough slack in the reins for Fred to stretch his head forward. This position, called the crest release, has two functions. One is to support your upper body to keep it from falling backward or farther forward. The other purpose is to keep your hands from jabbing Fred in the mouth while he jumps. Nothing—but *nothing*—sours a horse on jumping faster than being caught in the mouth.

As you approach the cross-rail, grasp a clump of mane with one of your index fingers. Sink your weight into your heels, absorbing the bouncing of the trot with your ankle and knee joints. Maintain your lower legs against Fred's sides. Aim for the center of the *X*, then focus your eyes straight ahead to a target beyond the fence, just as you did when you cantered ground rails.

The moment before take-off: The rider's hands on the horse's crest support his upper body. His weight is in his heels, his back is flat, and his eyes focused ahead.

Now's your chance to show how well you can do nothing. Simply hold your position and *wait* until you get to the fence. Or in terms of your perception, wait until the fence comes to you.

You'll feel the jump happen. The thrust of Fred's hindquarters leaving the ground will shove you forward and close your hip angle; the feeling will be the cantle of the saddle shoving your rear end. As you're pushed forward, you'll absorb that forward momentum by bending your elbows against Fred's neck. At the same time you'll let yourself sink down into the saddle as your horse jumps up underneath you.

A jump over a cross-rail lasts not much more than a second: Trot-trot-trot-*jump*-canter-canter. Yes, canter. Even after the lowest of cross-rails, Fred will canter away (he's been trained to do that).

Once you and Fred reach the other side of the fence, your job is to maintain your crest-release position for a stride or two. This ensures that you won't catch him in the mouth. Then open your hip angle and go back to your three-point full seat. Reestablish contact with Fred's mouth, canter in a straight line for a dozen strides or more, and then halt in a straight line.

This concept, known as riding out your line after a fence, is an important one. Fred needs to be reminded that although beginner riders

Leaving the ground, with the hands planted in a crest release.

may be in less than full control over and after a fence, that's no reason for him to exploit your vulnerability and do anything he feels like. When a second fence is added, you'll want Fred to be thinking about going directly to it, not ducking into the center of the ring or meandering anywhere else.

The landing: The rider's weight in her heels helps absorb the impact of landing.

By the way, just about all horses—and especially lesson horses—slow down when they're moving away from the gate end of a ring and speed up when heading toward the gate (after all, the gate is all that stands between them and their beloved barn or pasture). Approaching a cross-rail while you're going away from the gate may require more encouragement to Fred than one approached toward the gate.

Your instructor may have you take Fred over the X a half-dozen times or more. Each time you do, you'll get a better idea of the sensation of jumping. However, you're just as likely to discover one or more things that can go amiss.

Jumping Ahead of Your Horse

This problem is a result of your failing to do nothing during the approach and takeoff. Instead, you'll anticipate the jump and shove with your upper body or stand up in your stirrups. When Fred lands, you'll find your upper body splayed on his neck.

Solution: Keep your seat behind the pommel of the saddle and your weight in your heels. Wait for the jump to come to you, then allow the jump to happen—don't anticipate. Support your upper body with your hands—that's one of the reasons for the crest release. Remember, Fred does the jumping, you don't.

Tipping Forward

Your upper body ends up too far forward but not so exaggerated as in jumping ahead of your horse. This problem often occurs as a result of pivoting on your knee: Your legs slip, your heels come up, and you teeter forward.

Solution: Keep your weight in your heels and your lower legs on your horse's sides. The image of trying to touch your inner anklebones together through your horse's body can be helpful.

Leaning ahead into the jump, a common novice mistake, places too much of the rider's weight over the horse's forehand and encourages the horse to add an extra half-stride (known as "chipping") or to stop.

Being Left Behind

Being left behind is the opposite of jumping ahead of your horse. If your upper body falls behind your horse's center of balance when he leaves the

Another common beginner error, to fall behind the horse's motion, is known as being "left behind."

ground, you'll find yourself thrown backward into the air. Your hands will be sure to catch Fred in the mouth.

Solution: Maintain the half-seat with plenty of weight in your heels. And hold on to that pinch of mane.

Refusals

Horses stop at jumps, even little ones. They do so for a variety of reasons. A rider's upper body leaning too far forward places extra weight on the horse's forehand, which is often an invitation for a refusal. Lack of pace is another reason: Without enough pace and impulsion, a wise old school horse knows from bitter experience that he'll hit the jump. Accordingly, stopping becomes the wiser course of action (or inaction). Constantly being caught in the mouth will also discourage a horse.

Stops can happen quickly, but even if Fred grinds to a slow halt, you're likely to find yourself leaning up on his neck. When that happens, sit up, reorganize yourself, and then circle away from the fence and approach it again. This time add a little more pace or pay closer attention to your upper body's position during the approach. Your instructor, who has a ringside view of your position, will have some thoughts on the subject.

Assuming you aren't the cause, a second stop requires more stringent measures. If you're carrying a crop, one or two smart taps behind your leg should get Fred's attention either after the refusal or during the next approach to the fence. In some instances, your instructor may want to get on Fred to help him understand the error of his ways. That's not the worst thing in the world, and certainly no cause for embarrassment on your part. You did your job—it's Fred who needs a brief refresher course.

Run-Outs

The crest release is a trade-off: You're sacrificing rein contact for security. Some horses take advantage of that temporary loss of contact by swerving around the fence.

Run-outs can happen as fast as refusals do, and often much faster. Instead of coming to a halt in front of the fence, your horse will go around the fence either to the left or the right of it. You'll find yourself off balance, as if the horse had shied at something (in a sense, he did . . . he spooked at the fence).

Solution: Unlike refusals, which are remedied through leg aids, runouts call for hand corrections. If Fred ducked out to the right, pull him around with your left rein. If he ran out to the left, use your right rein. Use your legs to get his hindquarters around, too, but your hands are the primary aid. Then go back and try the fence again.

Many horses drift toward one side or the other while approaching a jump (and not just school horses—any number of top jumpers also have this propensity). If Fred is one of them, you may need to keep a stronger leg on the offending side and/or tap his shoulder with a crop during the approach.

Another technique involves the rein on the opposite side from where he drifts (the left rein if he goes to the right). Moving your hand a foot or so away from your body will create what's called an opening hand, used to guide a drifting horse back to the path. If you do use an

Run-outs invariably catch the novice rider by surprise. Once you've recovered your composure (and balance, if need be), you'll go back and try the fence again.

opening rein, be sure you're into your crest-release position by the time Fred reaches the takeoff spot.

An easier and often more effective cure for lesson-horse run-outs is more battlefield medicine than classical horsemanship: The instructor stands next to the fence on the side where the horse ran out. His or her presence and a sharp word or two is all it takes to remind the horse that fences are to be jumped, not avoided.

Rushing

Rushing a fence is the opposite of refusing to jump it. Instead of stopping, the horse hurries toward the jump as if impatient to get to the other side. That's because he *is* eager, usually because he's been caught in the mouth too often. Anticipating discomfort or outright pain, he reasons (so to speak) that he'd better get the jump over with as soon as possible.

The increase in pace often begins several strides before the fence. As a result, the novice rider is surprised and thrown out of balance. That leads to catching the horse in the mouth over the jump, which just reinforces the animal's instinct to hurry up and get away from the discomfort.

Often, though, rushing comes from a rider's confusing speed with impulsion. Remember the difference between speed (miles per hour) and impulsion (rpms). Building up excessive speed to the point that you're running a horse at a jump won't get him up and over. If anything, speed encourages a horse to become unbalanced. He'll end up too heavy on the forehand. That makes jumping more difficult; because instead of pushing himself—and you—over the fence with thrust from his hocks, he'll pull with his forelegs.

Solution: "Package" Fred and approach the fence with pace that comes from impulsion. You'll learn how much is enough from experience and your instructor's advice.

One solution is not to jump. If there's room, circle away from the fence as soon as Fred begins to rush. Done once or twice, circling reduces the chance that Fred will anticipate discomfort; it should help him keep an even pace up to and over the fence. But you won't want to pull him away from the fence only two or three strides from the jump, because that will teach him that it's okay to run out.

Curing a rusher usually takes skills that novice riders can't be expected to have. Your instructor may need to get on the horse and show, through tact and patience, that rushing is unnecessary.

Five Steps To Successful Jumping

This checklist for beginning jumping should become routine with practice:

1. *Impulsion and pace:* Establish your horse's impulsion (rpms) and pace (mph) during the approach to a fence, then maintain them down to the fence.
2. *Eye control:* Focus on a point beyond the jump.
3. *Jump the center of the fence.*
4. *Body and hand control:* Don't interfere with your horse from takeoff to landing. In particular, stay off his mouth.
5. *Follow-through:* Ride out the line after the fence to the focal point your eyes established during the approach.

11

MORE JUMPING

The most important principle is to want to do it, to be committed before you start off to getting to the other side of every fence every time.
—Captain Mark Phillips, *The Horse and Hound Book of Eventing*

Just as a journey of a thousand miles begins with a single step, that single cross-rail marks your introduction to jumping. You and Fred will go over it again and again, sometimes from the opposite direction, until your instructor is satisfied that you understand the basics of body position, pace, and timing.

A course is a series of fences, and the next step to learning how to jump a course is to add a second fence. Your instructor will erect it at a comfortable distance from the cross-rail—"comfortable" meaning a distance based on the length of Fred's cantering stride so that he need neither lengthen nor shorten his step.

The second jump may be a little spread fence (called an oxer) that measures 2 feet high by 2½ feet wide and is set (depending on the length of Fred's cantering stride) somewhere between 55 and 60 feet from the cross-rail.

You and Fred will begin your approach and trot the cross-rail just as you've been doing. You'll land cantering, but instead of stopping in a straight line, you'll stay in your two-point position with your hands on his crest. And as you do, you'll count strides.

Only full strides are counted, so you don't begin with Fred's landing. As he hits the ground, you'll say to yourself, "And . . ." Then when he takes his first complete stride, you'll continue with " . . . one," then "two-three" at the appropriate strides.

You'll keep your legs on Fred to maintain his pace and impulsion. Your eyes will focus on a distant point. If you feel he's not heading toward the center of the fence, you'll guide him there with your hands and legs (temporarily abandoning the crest release is permissible if you think Fred plans to run out).

At the count of "four," Fred will reach the oxer and leave the ground. Then—just as you did after jumping the single cross-rail—you'll canter away and halt in a straight line.

As you jump the X-to-oxer line several times, you'll find that not every approach, jump, or landing feels the same. That's where you'll use the tools you've developed earlier to make adjustments.

Suppose, for example, you generate too much impulsion trotting down to the X, and Fred jumps it with a bit too much enthusiasm. He'll land farther away from the cross-rail than he should, then canter on a bigger stride. If he were to continue at that pace, he'd reach the oxer in fewer than four strides. As a result, he'd be likely to add an extra, awkward, rider-jolting half stride known as a chip.

Or you might be tentative about your approach, and Fred virtually stepped over the cross-rail with little in the way of impulsion. To continue at that pace and with a short stride would get Fred to the vertical in five strides. He'd have to be a contortionist to fit in all five and *then* jump.

All that time you and Fred spent lengthening and shortening strides between ground poles (see page 99) will now pay off handsomely. If you sense that Fred jumped the cross-rail too "big," you can shorten his steps to fit in the four strides. Without abandoning your arm position for a generous crest release, you'll squeeze your hands on the reins or sit up slightly to open your hip angle, just as you did when you steadied Fred to get to a ground pole that was too far away.

On the other hand, as soon as you sense you'll get to the oxer in more than four strides, you'll close your legs on Fred's sides and perhaps add a cluck or two. Because you spent time during your warm-up getting Fred listening to your leg and staying in front of it, he'll be able to generate enough impulsion to open his stride. That's how he'll make up the difference between five wimpy strides and four good ones and then leave the ground for a quality jump.

Although cantering a fence feels very different from trotting one, your position should be no different. However, one problem that many beginners encounter is a loose lower leg. As often happens with cantering in general, the cause is gripping with thigh and knee. More weight in the heel to lengthen the leg is the solution here, too.

A word about flapping elbows: You close your legs at the girth to generate the impulsion and pace to make up lost ground. Flapping your elbows won't help. I mention this here because we all have a tendency to

Two flagrant errors: (1) looking down and (2) standing in the stirrups over the fence. (credit: Goobertone Photo)

use our elbows, in part because we see jockeys and movie cowboys try to hustle their horses along by flapping their wings in the Funky Chicken. The truth is that jockeys ride with their stirrups too short to let them use their legs, while movie cowboys flap because it's part of acting that they're in a hurry.

However, flapping elbows distract and disconcert horses that are about to jump. Flapping also encourages pulling back on the reins at a time when you want Fred to have unrestricted use of his head. Moral: Keep your elbows in.

Cantering both fences will not be very different from what you've been doing. Your instructor may have converted the cross-rail into a little vertical (a fence with no spread), since verticals, like oxers, call for a bit more respect in Fred's eye than a cross-rail does.

Just as when you trotted the *X*, you'll start by establishing a good pace and impulsion. Since the approach will probably take you on a track around one end of the ring, you'll make sure you're on the correct lead.

As you'll canter up to the fence at a steady pace, with your eyes up, heels down and hands on Fred's crest, you'll aim for the center of the rail. If it seems as though you'll be arriving too deep (or too long—a stride away from Fred's point of takeoff), you'll make the appropriate adjustment, just as you did while cantering ground rails or, more recently, cantering to the oxer. Of course, such judgment takes much practice to develop. More on this in the next section.

Although you won't do anything different during your approach and the jump itself, Fred will. Cantering strides cover more ground than trotting strides do, and Fred will land farther away from the vertical and with greater impulsion and pace than when trotting. But rather than steady him for the four strides, you'll ride the line in three strides. All that this requires is simply keeping your legs on him with your heels down and eyes up, and counting, "And [for the landing] . . . one . . . two . . . three," at which point you'll be airborne.

Your third jump may be set on a diagonal (see fences 3 and 7 in the diagram on p. 128). That's done for the specific purpose of teaching you how to approach a fence off a turn.

Many instructors make the first diagonal fence a trottable cross-rail (*X*) so that the new experience will be as easy as possible. Let's assume you'll take the fence after a left-hand turn.

You'll begin by cantering your first two jumps as usual. But instead of halting in a straight line, you'll take the downward transition to a trot, then trot around the end of the ring. To be able to steer, you'll abandon

---

A Word about Distances

You won't spend much time in the company of jumping riders and trainers without hearing about distances, good, bad, and ugly.

Horse-show hunter judges penalize horses and equitation judges penalize riders for leaving the ground too close or too far away from fences. Accordingly, instructors drill their students to develop a so-called eye for distances. Seeing a distance isn't really focusing your eyes on an object called a distance; it's the sense that you're a certain number of strides away from the jump.

Unfortunately, some instructors make a fetish out of demanding perfect distances. To hear them talk, leaving "too long" or "too deep" ranks with the Black Plague or the Decline of the West.

Don't become suckered into thinking that way. Everyone misses distances. Grand-prix-caliber riders occasionally leave too long or too deep, and we lesser mortals miss more frequently—especially beginners, who can't be expected to know where they and their horses are in relation to a fence without considerable experience (some riders are born with an natural eye, but don't count on it).

Developing an eye takes lots of practice. When you miss, learn from the experience. Did you fail to keep Fred at a consistent pace? Did he lose his impulsion or try to duck out? Did you lean up into the fence or drop your eyes and stare down at it, putting additional weight on Fred's forehand so that he threw in an extra step out of self-protection?

Whatever the reason, being embarrassed won't help. In the words of the legendary football coach Vince Lombardi, anyone who doesn't make mistakes just isn't trying hard enough.

---

your crest-release hand position, which you won't go back to until you're three or four strides from the new fence.

The goal is to line up the cross-rail so Fred can approach straight to its center and squarely (that is, at a right angle) to the fence. That will take some planning. If you cut the corner of the ring or come off the rail too soon, you'll jump the fence at a left-to-right angle. However, if you stay on the rail too long, you'll overshoot the middle of the fence and end up jumping right to left.

The trick is to line up the middle of the fence with something beyond it: a section or a post of the fence that encloses the ring, or a tree. Keep Fred on the rail (known as holding out) until you line up the center of the jump with the reference point you've chosen. Actually, you'll want to leave the rail a stride or two sooner to compensate for any centrifugal drift Fred makes while leaving the rail.

Lining up the two points takes some practice, but then again, so did learning to steer your car off the street and into a driveway. The good news is that once you've gotten the idea of lining up your jump, it will become second nature.

Arriving squarely—at a right angle—to the fence is particularly important. Jumping at an angle will encourage Fred to jump unevenly; he'll twist his body or lift one foreleg more than the other. A good image to keep in mind with regard to a square approach is a curved railroad track: Fred's "wheels" should stay on the curve, with his outside shoulder slightly ahead of his inside shoulder; when he reaches the fence, though, his shoulders should be square.

After you've trotted the fence to everyone's satisfaction, your instructor may turn the cross-rail into a vertical that you'll canter. Of course, you'll be certain to make sure Fred is on the correct lead around the turn.

If the third fence is more than four or five strides off the rail, you'll be making what's called a long approach. Problems with cantering long approaches are purely a mental matter. The longer it takes to get to a fence, the more time you have to change your mind. You may think, "Fred's going too fast . . . no, he's too slow . . . we'll get there too long . . . no, too close . . . no, too—I don't know!"

The solution: Shut up and wait! Maintain your pace, which—if it's a steady and active one (that's *active,* not hurried)—will give you a workable distance. Problems arise only when you start making multiple adjustments in the spirit of the Three Stooges' "I got it! I got it!—I don't got it!"

Once you can jump fences both on a straight line and off a turn, you can theoretically tackle any hunter or horsemanship course in the world.* That's all those courses are—series of verticals and oxers connected by straight lines and turns.

You'll discover this fact as your instructor adds on fences. Typical courses involve lines along the long sides of the ring and up and/or down the diagonal, such as the classic eight-fence hunter side-diagonal-side-diagonal. Some diagonal fences will involve a long approach, while others will be set only a few strides off the track of the ring. But whatever and wherever the obstacles are placed, you can be certain your instructor will set them on comfortable, encouraging distances for Fred and you.

As you progress, your timing and balance will improve, and you'll come to rely less and less on the long crest release. Instead of planting your hands and grabbing a clump of mane, you'll carry your hands to follow Fred's mouth to the base of the jump, then slide them only a foot or more up his crest as he leaves the ground. That technique gives you greater control over the reins and, through them, over Fred.

How long it takes you to reach the point where you can safely and comfortably negotiate a complete course of eight fences will depend on your abilities. It will also depend on the frequency of your lessons and how much you practice.

With regard to practice, anyone bitten by the jumping bug will want to jump at every possible opportunity. That's not a good idea, and for several reasons. First, few if any stables permit unsupervised jumping. Although you may be able to rent Fred for riding on the flat in the ring or

---

*Jumper courses involve combinations—two or three fences one to three strides strides apart—and bending lines that also present tricky options in striding. That's all beyond the scope of this little treatise—see Chapter 16 for books and videos on the subject.

taking him out on the trail, the two of you won't be able to pursue independent studies over fences. Too many problems can happen without the supervision of a qualified person, not the least of which would be your jumping the legs off Fred.

You see, too many jumps—even over low fences—take their toll on a horse. It's said that a horse has only a certain number of jumps in him. If that's right, it's certainly true for lesson horses. Kindness and good sense dictate that you keep Fred happy and sound by jumping him only during lessons, especially on days when other riders are also scheduled to ride him.

That's not to say that you can't work on jumping skills between lessons. Remember those ground poles? Just because you're jumping real fences now doesn't mean you can't benefit from them. One ground pole in the center of the ring can be cantered in figure eights—a great way to practice jumping off a short turn. You can also set two ground poles at distances where you can leave out or add strides by lengthening or shortening your horse's stride. And in neither case will you be putting stress on his legs in the process.

Jumping the center of the fence is correct, but pivoting on your knee proclaims a loose lower leg. (credit: Goobertone Photo)

It should go without saying (but I'll say it anyway) that jumping during a trail ride is the height—or depth—of foolishness. That log lying off the trail may be no higher or wider than the oxer you jumped during your last lesson, but there's a critical difference. Fences made of rails set in cups on standards come down when a horse's feet hit them. Logs don't yield, and if Fred happens to take off badly (the footing may be slippery, for example), he can injure his leg or even flip over if he hits the log.

There's plenty of opportunity for cross-country jumping if and when you become involved with foxhunting, hunter pacing, or combined training. Until then, stick to the trail. And for jumping, stick to your barn's ring . . . and perhaps a horse show.

12

YOUR FIRST HORSE SHOW

The child who is fortunate enough to be associated with horses during his formative years can look back on fond memories, and those who continue to ride, hunt, or show during their lifetime seldom experience anything more gratifying than the thrill of winning their first ribbon.
—Stephen Hawkins, in *Learning to Ride,*
Hunt, and Show by Gordon Wright

Competition can do strange things to people. Quiet, unassuming souls who are normally bundles of self-doubt can turn into raging bulls of assertiveness the moment they set foot on a horse-show grounds. Conversely, some of the most self-assured and confident lesson or trail riders would rather remove their own gallbladders without anesthesia than sign up for a show. You just never can tell.

Even if you don't have a competitive bone in your body, showing has benefits above and beyond the chance to win brightly colored ribbons, admiration, and/or envy. Lessons are a fine opportunity for supervised instruction, but a horse show places you in situations where you're forced to apply your skills without an instructor's help. Lessons are the textbook, but horse shows are the test.

If and when something goes wrong during a lesson, your trainer will shout out a correction or the two of you can engage in a Socratic dialogue to analyze and solve the problem. That's not the way horse shows work. Once you're in the ring, you're on your own. Whatever happens, it's up to you, and you alone, to cope. And when you do, you can take justifiable pride in the ability to think on your feet—no, make that *seat.*

A horse show is also an excellent way to measure your progress. Although you may feel confident that you've corrected a loose lower leg, a rounded back, or heavy hands on the reins, seeing what the judge of a horsemanship class has to say in that regard is a better test. Maybe six months ago you couldn't remember a pattern of jumps even if the course diagram were tattooed on your wrist. An over-fences class will show you how much more ring savvy you've acquired.

And if you *do* have a competitive bone in your body, you'll be in hog heaven. The sense of pride and accomplishment you'll experience when you're handed a top prize ribbon, especially one that's blue in color, will make you feel 10 feet tall even if you're not sitting on a horse at the time.

A suitable place for your horse-show debut may be no farther away than the stable where you take lessons or just down the road from where your backyard lesson horse lives. Many riding academies hold small, informal competitions for their customers and other people in the neighborhood. The events are called schooling shows, because they were originally designed as places where young horses could be schooled, or made accustomed, to competition. They're also unrated, which means that the rules of the American Horse Shows Association (horse sports' national governing body) or any breed or discipline organization don't apply.

Organizers of schooling shows do everything possible to make the experience encouraging for riders as well as horses. Individual events are called classes, and there will be at least one class for every age and level of riding skill. Beginners aged 12 and under compete in the "short stirrup" division,* while the "long stirrup" division is for novice adults over 18. Riders in between enter "maiden horsemanship" classes for those who've never won a ribbon, then move up to the novice, limit, and open levels as they continue their winning ways.

Schooling shows hire judges for their attitude as much as for their expertise. The judges are chosen because they understand what first-time or occasional competitors go through, emotionally as well as physically. They also understand the limitations of lesson horses. On more than one occasion during one particular schooling show, I saw a judge move from the middle of the ring—where judges usually stand—to position himself behind a reluctant school horse and then cluck and slap his clipboard to help the rider get the animal over a jump.

Just as important, schooling-show judges are encouraged to write brief comments about each rider on their scoring cards. Unlike more formal and more demanding shows, the cards are made public after the class. The comments are positive ("excellent use of eyes") as well as constructively critical ("don't look down to find diagonals and leads"). You'll learn as much from these remarks as from any other type of lesson situation.

Another appealing feature of schooling shows is that they don't require a tremendous financial investment. A class usually costs less than an average riding lesson, plus you seldom have the expense of shipping a horse to the show: If Fred doesn't live at the barn that's holding the show, you can ride him down the road to the event.

If you want to be serious about apparel, English show clothes consist of boots and breeches (jodhpurs and jodhpur boots for youngsters), a shirt and tie for men and boys, a collarless "ratcatcher" shirt with choker collar for women and girls, and a dark riding coat for both genders. Hard hunt caps with chin harnesses are, of course, as essential for showing as for lessons.

---

*A division is a group of related classes. The beginner adult horsemanship division, for instance, might consist of one flat and two over-fences classes.

Although schooling shows tend to be informal events, riders can take the opportunity to dress up if they wish. (credit: Goobertone Photo)

Western riders wear western boots, jeans with or without chaps, a long-sleeve shirt with or without neckerchief, and a western hat.

However, you needn't go out and buy formal show clothes if you don't want to. Not everyone wears them, and schooling-show judges don't care whether you wear boots and breeches, chaps or just plain pants. It's your performance that counts.

However, whether you buy or borrow items or just wear whatever you wear for lessons, you'll want to take pains to make sure your clothes are neat and clean.

Classes for beginning riders are usually placed early in the horse-show schedule, if not first. That means you're likely to be at the show by the dawn's early light. Your first stop will be at the stable office or the show secretary's stand, where you'll pay your entry fee and receive your number (judges identify riders by numbers on the signs they wear on their backs). If there's time to warm up, take advantage of the opportunity to stretch Fred's and your muscles. Don't overdo it, though. Fred may have a long day ahead if lots of other riders will use him in their own classes.

That also applies to Fred if he's a private horse (people at the stable will groom lesson horses and clean their tack). You, his owner—or the other riders who may be riding him in the show—will want to spend the day before and/or the morning of the show grooming him. Take the time to clean his tack, too. A well-turned-out horse is the sign of good horsemanship, and although you won't win any bonus points for a well-groomed horse, making a good impression on the judge won't hurt your chances.

Sharing Horses

A few decades ago the Bermuda Equestrian Federation invited a group of American three-day event riders to take part in an annual horse show. Also invited was Jimmy Elder, who represented Canada as both a show-jumping and a three-day Olympic rider. The guests were assigned horses by their hosts and captained teams of local riders. Elder's team included a youngster who owned a small horse barely out of the pony-sized category, and since Elder is on the small side, he was given the animal, too.

One get-acquainted session was all it took for Elder to realize that the horse needed help. And so he spent much of the day before the competition schooling the horse and working with the owner to get their program together.

The next morning Elder gave the horse a good last-minute school before the show started. But when the horse's owner competed before he did, her indecisive riding undid all the schooling that Elder had completed. When his turn came, Elder gave the crowd a wonderful lesson in Schooling-In-The-Show-Ring 101, but the result was pretty much of a stalemate.

Moral: A horse is only as good as his last ride.

Even the most placid Valium-on-four-legs is likely to come alive at a horse show, especially if the show is not where the animal lives. The sights and sounds of horses, riders, and spectators will draw Fred's attention and make him more alert to these unfamiliar distractions. Other horses may become more agitated, so watch out for flattened ears and cocked hooves while you're standing or walking behind them. Other riders will be preoccupied with their upcoming classes, so don't assume everyone is as aware of potential equine misbehavior as you are.

You're more likely to have the services of a trainer (proper horse-show lingo for "instructor") if Fred is privately owned. After all, his owner has a vested interest in his well-being, certainly during the first time you and he go horse-showing. That's all to the good if Fred's owner happens to be your teacher.

But if you ride at a public stable and your teacher is involved in the show as ringmaster or show secretary, you may be pretty much on your own—or at least without the benefit of undivided attention for last-minute and between-rounds advice from a familiar voice.

That's not to say you can't find help. Schooling shows being informal and good-natured affairs, riders often volunteer advice to friends and even to strangers. Sometimes the advice is unsolicited, but it's no less welcome. In one of my first shows, I was blithely posting up a storm in what I considered superlative form when from among the spectators lining the rail I heard a small voice call out, "Steve, bounce once." A youngster who took lessons at the barn had come to my diagonal-impaired rescue, bless her 10-year-old heart.

No matter how you feel about competition, sooner or later nerves will rear their ugly head. "Why am I doing this?" is a question on the minds, if not the lips, of many first-timers. "I don't know how to ride . . . I'll embarrass myself and my trainer . . . I must be crazy." Veterans are not immune from such doubts. A Fact of Life: Everyone suffers from horse-show jitters to some extent, from a small swarm of butterflies in the belly to major mental rigor mortis.

If you anticipate coming down with a case of horse-show nerves, you might want to discuss the matter with your instructor in advance of the show. Most instructors had the same experience when they started their own show careers, and they'll suggest antidotes. The condition being pandemic, lots of books on the subject offer helpful approaches (see Further Information in the back of this book). And let me add my two cents' worth.

Waiting to go into the ring, especially sitting on your horse at the in gate waiting for your turn in an over-fences class, gives you plenty of time to think. And to worry. And especially to try to remember everything you'll want to do. That last one is a recipe for disaster, the equivalent of cramming for an exam as you walk into the test classroom. Besides, you'll find yourself dwelling on everything that can go wrong.

As you wait to go into the ring, take a few deep breaths. Inhale slowly and exhale slowly, as if you're expelling all the bad thoughts and physical tension in your body.

While you're breathing, try to visualize all the ways things can go right. In your mind's eye, you'll see Fred walking, trotting, and cantering with rhythm and pace . . . you sitting tall and with a deep seat, picking up correct diagonals and leads . . . what an impressive performance.

Sports psychologists have a term for this technique: *imaging.* By creating images of the way you'd like the ride to go, you're creating a positive role model. Then when you get into the ring, you can try to match those images and achieve a self-fulfilling prophecy.

Although deep breathing and positive imaging won't themselves guarantee success, they're a heck of a lot better than dwelling on disaster.

Whether your first class is called equitation or horsemanship, the criteria are the same: The judge will be considering the riders' form and control.

The first direction in flat classes is traditionally to the right, so Fred and the other horses will start out moving clockwise around the ring. Until the ringmaster tells the judge, "Here's your class," or tells the class, "You're now being judged," you can work at will. You might want to try a little trot to help Fred establish an active pace, and you can get up into a half-seat to stretch your legs and heels—you decide. But don't crowd anyone or run up the rump of the horse in front of you.

Once the judging begins, the ringmaster or the judge will tell you when and what to do. By tradition, everyone first walks, then trots (or jogs), and—if the class calls for all three gaits—canters (or lopes). Because the transition to the canter is made from the walk, the sequence works out to be walk, trot, walk, and then canter.

In some instances the judge may ask only a few riders at a time to canter, in an effort to avoid a cavalry charge or traffic jam. Those who aren't cantering will wait their turns in the center of the ring.

At the command "reverse, please," you and Fred will make a 180-degree turn or reverse through the center of the ring. You'll then repeat the walk-trot-and-possibly-canter sequence moving to the left.

Some Hard-Earned, Ring-Savvy Advice

- The judge can't reward your efforts if he or she can't see you. Position yourself so other horses don't obscure the judge's view of you and Fred.
- By the same token, don't try so hard to be seen that you pose a threat. That includes cutting off other horses or running down the judge. Most judges stand in the middle of the ring; the official won't think much of your horsemanship if Fred knocks him or her down.
- Use the ring to advantage. Suppose Fred is reluctant to take his right lead. Rather than risk getting on the wrong lead right in front of the judge, position yourself so you're behind the judge when the class is asked to canter (you can pretty easily anticipate the command, which comes after the trot-to-walk sequence). Getting behind the judge by circling through the middle of the ring is perfectly acceptable and also a good way to get out of traffic jams.
- Make smooth transitions between gaits. You won't win any bonus points by moving from the canter to the trot a split second after the ringmaster calls out, "Trot, please," if the transition is abrupt and sloppy. First organize yourself and Fred, and then make the transition.
- The importance of breathing can't be overemphasized. You know why and you know how. Enough said.
- Picking up the wrong diagonal or the wrong lead isn't the end of the world. Neither is losing a stirrup (it would be grounds for elimination in an AHSA-sanctioned equitation class, but schooling shows are more lenient). Just correct the error and continue. Besides, the judge might have missed it, or other horses or riders in the class might make more critical errors.
- Put a workmanlike expression on your face. Looking the part of a capable and confident rider is all part of showmanship. The judge may think you know more than you do. On the other hand, frowning or looking as though you're about to burst into tears invites the judge to consider that you don't like something about your riding. Don't give the judge a chance to agree.

As the class ends, the ringmaster will ask all the riders to line up their horses side by side in the middle of the ring and facing in a particular direction. The judge will then walk behind the horses, double-checking his or her notes against the numbers on the riders' backs. You will continue to sit up, keeping your good position in the saddle. Nor will you turn and start chatting with your neighbor. That's because the class is still being judged. Only when the judge has handed his or her scorecard to the ringmaster or has left the ring can you relax.

Or perhaps the judge hasn't made up his or her mind about one or more of the placings. He or she may ask two or more riders to return to the rail for additional work. If you're called, ride your best. If you're not called, you don't become upset, because you did your best . . . and you might still win a good prize.

When the ribbon winners are announced and the ribbons handed out, women and girls smile and nod to the person who presents them the ribbon. Men and boys remove their caps or hats and smile. All recipients say thank you.

The judge's card will be posted on a bulletin board or otherwise made available after the class. Read the comments in the company of your instructor if you can, and take the remarks to heart. Such comments as "loose lower leg" and "rounded back" indicate things to work on in your lessons and practicing. Remarks like "good hands" and "prompt canter pickups" show the progress you've made. Either way, you'll learn something useful.

Over-fences classes usually follow all the flat classes, because setting up and removing standards and rails is a time-consuming drag. If you and Fred are jumping, you'll discover that schooling-show courses are uncomplicated. They range from twice-around and egg-rolls to hunter-course permutations of outside and diagonal lines (see illustration). Course diagrams will be posted on a bulletin board. If your class calls for anything more complicated than twice around the ring, memorize the order in which you'll jump the fences.

Ten minutes or so before your class, get on Fred (if he's not being used). A few minutes of relaxed riding on the flat in a warm-up ring

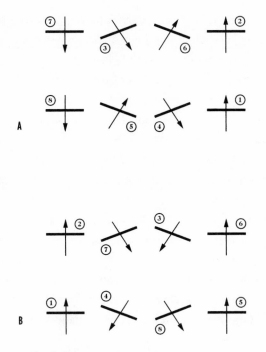

Two simple hunter courses

might be followed—if your instructor is available to supervise—by trotting a cross-rail once or twice and then cantering a little vertical. Then walk to the show ring's in gate and wait.

Some schooling shows post the order in which horses will jump. Many don't, though; riders can go whenever they feel like going. If the latter is the case, there's no compelling reason to be the first (unless your nerves can't stand the thought of waiting and you want to get it over with). The point of waiting is have the chance to watch others go. As you watch, you'll ride the course in your mind. You'll think about pace and impulsion and the track between fences you'll want Fred to take.

When your turn comes, you'll enter the ring at a brisk walk, then start your opening trot-to-canter circle. That circle is important, because that's how you'll build up the pace and impulsion to take you to the first fence.

Then you'll just jump the jumps the way you do at home. Fred will canter at an energetic (but not hurried) pace, and you'll guide him along

The jumps in beginner over-fences classes are low and straightforward. (credit: author)

the track from fence to fence. You'll use your corners (that is, not cut them too sharply) to make your turns. Changes of direction will be accompanied by simple changes of lead without Fred losing his pace.

And you'll breathe all the way around the course.

If Fred chips in front of a fence, forget about it—after all, it's only one fence and, besides, there's nothing you can do about it after it happens. If you lose a stirrup or have a run-out or go off course, fix the problem and continue. If Fred stops at a fence, circle and reestablish your pace; even if from a trot, Fred *will* get to the other side.

End your round with a closing circle near the gate. That's to make a smooth downward transition from the canter through the trot to the walk. Then leave the ring. And no matter what happened in the ring, pat your horse and smile. That attitude is called showmanship.

Prize ribbons will be handed out after the final horse goes. Sometimes winners ride into the ring for their awards, sometimes they walk in while a trainer or a spectator holds their horse. Women nod, men remove caps or hats, and everyone says thank you. The judge's card will be posted and you can read the comments.

In addition to equitation classes on the flat and over fences, schooling shows hold other events in which beginners can take part.

In pleasure classes, the judge will award top ribbons to horses that exhibit comfortable gaits and a pleasant attitude. You'll show at the walk, trot (or jog), and canter (or lope) in both directions, then stand quietly and perhaps back a few steps. If you're taking Fred in such a class, ride him on a reasonably loose (but not floppy) rein to show he's a relaxed, happy guy that doesn't need to be muscled around the ring. Smiling is to be encouraged—oh, that Fred, such a pleasure!

Pairs classes are what the name suggests: two horses to a team, ridden side by side at the walk and trot (whether to canter is at the discretion of show management). Top prizes go to horses that match in size and color as well as a similar style of movement. Hint: To stay stirrup to stirrup, the outside horse will have farther to travel and, therefore, must move faster than the inside horse.

A trail class replicates the kinds of skills needed to negotiate a trail ride. One at a time, horse and rider step over a low fence or log, open and close a gate, and walk through a chute made of ground poles. Fred may have to stand quietly while you put on a raincoat, remove a letter from a mailbox, and/or dismount and remount. The number and type of obstacles is up to the judge or the show's manager; the course will be posted ahead of time.

Trail classes at schooling shows are meant to be lots of fun, and judges often contribute to the entertainment. That happened in one such class at the end of a long day of showing when we were asked to dismount and lead our horses over a little cross-rail. As my horse stepped and I hopped over the jump, the judge told the crowd, "Ladies and gentlemen—the best fence they had all day!"

Other "fun" classes include Spoon-and-Potato, in which competitors walk and trot while balancing a potato on a soup spoon. The last one to drop the spud wins. The Lucky Buck is sometimes done bareback: Riders hold a dollar bill between their knee and the horse. The last one to let the money slip out after walking, trotting, and cantering gets to keep the proceeds (who says you can't make money in the horse-show game!).

Even though you may have arrived early in the day and showing has taken its physical and emotional toll, make every effort to stay to watch more advanced riders compete. They'll appreciate your support. From your perspective, you'll be able to see where continuing with lessons and gaining riding "mileage" can take you.

Horse-show ribbons and their placings:

First prize = blue
Second = red
Third = yellow
Fourth = white
Fifth = pink
Sixth = green
Seventh = purple
Eighth = brown
Ninth = gray
Tenth = light blue

At the conclusion of each division, the division championship is computed. Winning a class is worth (usually) 5 points, second place 3 points, and third place 1 point. The competitor who scores highest is the champion and receives a tricolor ribbon of blue, red, and yellow. The second highest placing is the reserve champion and wins a tricolor ribbon of red, yellow, and white.

13

THE WORLD OF
HORSE SPORTS

I've spent most of my life riding horses.
The rest of the time I just wasted.
—Anonymous

One of the many reasons that horses make such wonderful "sports equipment" is their versatility. Golf clubs for are suitable just for golf, and tennis racquets are suitable just for tennis (okay, "The Odd Couple"'s Oscar Madison used one for draining spaghetti), but horses are vehicles that take riders to a wide range of activities.

You've discovered some of them so far, but if you are skilled enough to trail ride and participate in an entry-level horse show, you ride well enough to take part in many more of them, and you certainly have the tools to develop the requisite skills for others.

Most of these disciplines require horses that have been specially trained for the particular activity. Fred hasn't been, so you may be obliged to bid him a fond farewell and move on to another animal. But rest assured, your old pal should still be available for occasional trail rides during which the two of you can reminisce about the old days.

Which activities to try depends entirely on your interests and resources. Western riders may want to stay on that side of the pasture, and the same for English riders, but I'd encourage everyone at least to become familiar with what's out there. Although you may never go on a hunter pace or sit on a cutting horse or swing a polo mallet, you might find yourself learning to appreciate and admire the horsemanship involved in those and other sports. You owe it to yourself find out as much about the breadth of horse sports as you can.

The following brief and far-from-complete description of activities can do no more than hint at their flavor and appeal. Neither can watching them on TV, although the sights and sounds coupled with expert commentary will go a long way toward acquainting you with the basic rules and some of the strategies and subtleties. As the saying goes, check your local listings to see what's available (breed and discipline organization magazines and Web sites often alert readers to dates and times that programs will be telecast).

Magazines, newspapers, and Web sites will also alert you to events in your area. So will notices and ads on tack shop bulletin boards, and word of mouth around stables. Since the best way to learn about particular activities is as an on-site spectator, plan to attend. If you can go in the company of someone who's familiar with the sport, so much the better. If not, don't hesitate to ask people questions when you're there at the horse show, polo match, horse trial, or the reining or cutting or penning. In return you'll get valuable insights into what you're watching as well as suggestions about how to get started as a participant.

HORSE SHOWS

There's far more to horse showing than the long stirrup division. Many English-style riders progress to more demanding equitation divisions. Thousands of juniors (18 years old and under) spend much of the show year trying to qualify for such national titles as the ASPCA Maclay held at New York City's National Horse Show, the AHSA Hunter-Seat Medal

Behind the scenes at a horse show.

at the Pennsylvania National Show in Harrisburg, Pennsylvania, and the USET Finals at the U.S. Equestrian Team's headquarters in Gladstone, New Jersey, as well as at the Flintridge Riding Club in Flintridge, California. All take place in the fall of the year.

Equitation divisions for adults are growing in popularity. Many competitors learned their craft as Medal/Maclay riders, but others started riding when they were well out of the junior ranks.

Hunter Classes

The hunter division focuses on horses that exhibit graceful form and the jumping style based on the sport of foxhunting. Judges in over-fences classes look for a balanced form in the air, with forelegs lifted high and even and hind legs under the horse's hindquarters. Hunter courses are no more complicated than the combinations of outside and diagonal lines you and Fred have faced. They range in height from 2½ to 4 feet, with 3 and 3½ being most popular with amateur riders.

Judges of hunter under-saddle classes (informally called hacks) give high marks to horses with long, low ground-covering strides at the walk, trot, and canter.

135

To do well in the hunter division requires a horse that jumps in form and is also a nice mover across the ground. You'll also need a fairly accurate eye for seeing distances, since a horse will jump his best when he arrives at the optimum takeoff point in front of every fence.

Jumper Classes

Form on the part of horse or rider isn't taken into account in jumper classes, the most exciting of English-style horse-show events. All you have to do is jump the fences in the correct order without knocking them down and get around the course within the time allowed. Knocking fences down or refusing to jump them incurs penalty points called faults: 4 faults for each knockdown, 3 faults for the first refusal, 6 more for a second stop at the same or a later fence, and elimination after a third. In addition, time faults are given for exceeding the time within which the horse must complete the course.

Some jumper events are "speed" classes, in which knockdowns are converted into seconds added to the actual time it took to complete the course. The fastest horse is the winner. If the class follows a jump-off format and two or more horses finish with the same lowest score, a second round (the jump-off) adds the element of excitement. Competitors go in their original order over a shorter and twistier course, with the fastest times determining the final placings in case horses are still tied.

Although most people think of grand-prix-type fences in excess of 4 or 5 feet in height when they think of show jumping, you'll be relieved to learn that those in entry-level jumper classes are considerably lower. If you and your horse can safely negotiate 3 to 3½ feet at a good pace, you'll be competitive. If you leave the jumps up, that is.

For Further Information

The American Horse Shows Association (AHSA) is the governing body of horse shows. Membership, which includes a copy of its rule book, is essential for anyone planning to compete in rated events.

American Horse Shows Association
4047 Iron Works Parkway
Lexington, KY 40511
phone (606) 258-2472
fax (606) 231-6662
www.ahsa.org

New York office:
220 East 42nd Street
New York, NY 10017
phone (212) 972-2472
fax (212) 983-7286

Approximately 200 colleges and universities from coast to coast belong to the Intercollegiate Horse Show Association (IHSA). Owning a horse is unnecessary; riders compete in English or Western classes on mounts furnished by the host event. Success throughout the year qualifies students (and alumni) for regional shows and the academic-year-end national finals.

Intercollegiate Horse Show Association
P.O. Box 741
Stony Brook, NY 11790-0741
phone (516) 751-2803
fax (516) 751-1157

Western horse shows offer far more in the way of divisions. Most are based on actual ranch work, but events like pole bending and barrel racing started out as—and remain—plain flat-out fun.

Reining Classes

Reining classes are inspired by ranch work. Horses perform a predetermined sequence of movements, with the judges announcing the pattern beforehand. Among the movements are circles and figure eights with flying changes of lead. Another is the run-down, where the horse gallops down the centerline or along the rail from one end of the arena to the

A sliding stop performed in a reining class. (Photo by Wyatt McSpadden courtesy of the American Quarter Horse Association.)

other. Run-downs often end with a sliding stop, a spectacular movement in which the horse's hindquarters seem to melt into the ground as he comes to a straight halt (his hind legs will send up a cloud of the ring's footing). The rollback calls for a 180-degree turn on the haunches followed by loping away, the entire movement done in one fluid motion. In the spin, the horse's inside hind foot remains pivoted on the ground while the horse turns one or more complete circles.

Reining is scored on the basis of each movement. Each horse starts at 70 points; a full or a half point is added or deducted according to how well the movement was performed.

In addition to finding reining classes at Western horse show, entire events are devoted to the sport, which recently became the first Western discipline of the United States Equestrian Team.

For Further Information

National Reining Horse Association
3000 Northwest 10th Street
Oklahoma City, OK 73107-5302
phone (405) 946-7400

fax (405) 946-8410

www.nrha.com

Calf Roping Classes

Calf roping is a real partnership between a cowboy and his horse. When it's done at rodeos, the fastest time to rope and tie a calf determines the winner. In horse shows, however, the horse is judged on how well he responds to his rider's cues and how well he reacts on his own.

Once the calf is released from a pen, a well-trained roping horse smoothly moves up on the calf's tail. Speeding up or slowing down to maintain this position, called rating, is something the horse does on his own, without the rider's cueing.

The same sliding stop you'll see in reining classes happens once the rider ropes the calf. While the rider dismounts and runs toward the calf, the horse backs up to keep tension on the rope until the roper throws the calf.

It goes without saying that any horse that takes part in roping events or classes needs special training. So does the rider.

Calf roping—The rider dismounts swiftly as the horse keeps tension on the rope. (Photo by Wyatt McSpadden courtesy of the American Quarter Horse Association).

Dally Team Roping Classes

Dally team roping takes its name from the Spanish phrase *de la vuelta,* which refers to taking a turn of a rope around the saddle horse. It's a team sport in which one roper catches a steer by the head and the other by the animal's feet.

The event is really one or the other of two classes. In heading, the horse whose rider ropes the steer's head is judged; in heeling, the horse that carries the rider who ropes the hind legs is scored.

In both calf roping and dally team roping, horses are scored between 60 and 80 points, with 70 counting as average work. In addition, team ropings where speed is the criterion are very popular and throughout all parts of the country.

For Further Information

United States Team Roping Championships
7511 Fourth Street Northwest
Albuquerque, NM 87107
or
P.O. Box 7651
Albuquerque, NM 87194
phone (505) 899-1870
fax (505) 897-9743
www.ustrc.com

Cutting Horses

The job of the cutting horse is to prevent a cow that is separated, or cut, from the herd from returning to the herd. What's more, the horse does it with no assistance from his rider.

Each round, or work, lasts 2½ minutes. At the sound of the buzzer, the rider (known as a cutter) walks his or her horse into the herd and chooses the cow for his or her horse to work. Then the cutter drops the reins and lets the horse take over.

A cutting horse works a cow. (Photo by Wyatt McSpadden courtesy of the American Quarter Horse Association.)

It's the cow's herd instinct versus the horse's cow sense—his ability to anticipate the cow's every move. Moving from side to side, the horse stays between the cow and the herd while the cutter braces against the saddle horn and plays spectator.

If the cow stops trying to get back to the herd, the cutter has the option, if time allows, of working a second cow. You'll find cutting at large Western shows and shows, called cuttings that exclusively feature cutting classes and in which large prize purses reflect the sport's popularity and prosperity.

If you haven't seen a cutting horse drop down and stare a cow eye to eye, then move with the agility of a ballet dancer or a middle linebacker, you're missing out on one of the most extraordinary sights in the horse world. Even better, take up an offer to ride a cutting horse (push against the saddle horn to brace yourself—pulling on the horn just yanks you out of the saddle). Then stay aboard and enjoy the view from what cutters call "the best seat in the house."

For Further Information

National Cutting Horse Association
4704 Highway 377 South
Fort Worth, TX 76116-8805

phone (817) 244-6188
fax (817) 244-2015

Team Penning

Team penning blends horsemanship and teamwork. The object is to separate three cows (identified by numbers painted on their backs) from a large herd gathered at one end of the arena, then move them into a pen at the other end. Each team consists of three riders, and each member has an assigned job. One cuts the designated cows and moves them up to a teammate who herds them into the pen. The third rider keeps the cows from escaping back to the herd. But these roles can and do change, and since everyone needs to know what everyone is doing and where, there's constant shouting up and down the arena.

Each team has a maximum of two minutes to pen its cows, with the fastest times determining the winners. A team that pens all three will place higher than one that pens only two, while two penned cattle will beat only one.

Events for team penning are held throughout the year and all over the country. One reason for the sport's growth is that just about any re-

Signaling to the judges at the end of a successful team-penning round. (Photo by Wyatt McSpadden courtesy of the American Quarter Horse Association.)

sponsive horse can be used. Another is that families enjoy competing as a team.

For Further Information

United States Team Penning Association
P.O. Box 161848
Fort Worth, TX 76161-1848
phone (800) 848-3882
fax (817) 232-4771

Barrel Racing

Barrel racing takes place at both horse shows and rodeos. Once associated with young girls, it is now widely popular with riders of both genders and all ages.

The course, which consists of three barrels set in a triangular pattern, is run in a cloverleaf pattern, usually starting by circling the barrel to

Barrel racing (Photo by Wyatt McSpadden courtesy of the American Quarter Horse Association.)

the right. A five-second penalty for any barrel the horse or rider knocks over is added to the actual time it takes to complete the course.

To be competitive, you'll need a horse that can do his flying changes, turn on a dime, and run fast.

For Further Information

National Barrel Horse Association
P.O. Box 1988
Augusta, GA 30901-1988
phone (706) 722-RACE
fax (706) 722-9575

Dressage

Dressage is a French word usually translated as "training." However, dressage is more than simply schooling a horse. It is the systematic improvement of responsiveness and athletic ability according to centuries-old principles and exercises.

Dressage competitions require horse-and-rider teams to perform a test composed of a series of movements (in that way, it's very similar to Western reining). The arena in which the tests are performed is marked by letters around its perimeter plus an imaginary *X* that marks its center. The movements of the test are described in terms of these letters, such as, "Enter at *A* at the walk, halt at *X*."

Tests at lower levels include the walk, trot, and canter, as well as the halt. Higher levels add collection and extensions, such lateral movements as the half-pass (where the horse moves simultaneously forward and to the side) and flying changes of lead. The most advanced tests contain two examples of a highly collected trot: the passage (pronounced "pah-sahz"), in which the horse appears to float across the arena; and the piaffe ("pee-aff"), in which he literally trots in place.

Scores range from 10 (perfect) to 0 (not performed) and are given for each movement. The higher end of the scale goes to well-performed gaits and prompt and accurate transitions between the gaits.

A dressage test at a national competition. (credit: author).

No reasonably balanced and responsive horse would be out of place in a low-level dressage test. In fact, many people use dressage tests to monitor their horse's training progress.

For Further Information

United States Dressage Federation
P.O. Box 6669
Lincoln, NE 68506-0669
phone (402) 434-8550
fax (402) 434-8570

Combined Training

Combined training, often called eventing, was inspired by the qualities of obedience, boldness, and endurance needed in a cavalry horse. These qualities are demonstrated in the sport's three phases. Each horse-and-rider combination begins with a dressage test. Then they negotiate a multimile cross-country jumping course of permanent obstacles (translation: the solid

145

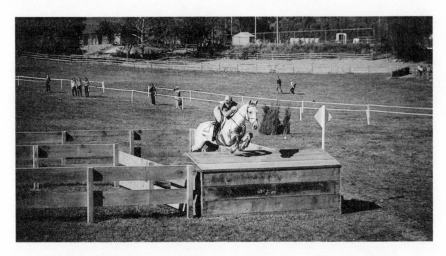

Negotiating a cross-country obstacle at a three-day event (credit: author).

fences don't come down when hit). A show-jumping course is the final phase, intended to test whether the horse has enough energy left after the cross-country. Scores from all three phases determine the prizewinners.

A very athletic, fit, and brave horse is essential for the upper reaches of three-day eventing (the most advanced competitions hold each of the three phases on consecutive days). The rider needs to be brave, too—galloping at speed for approximately 4 miles across uneven cross-country terrain and over those jumps isn't for the faint of heart.

However, any horse that's responsive on the flat and a reasonably fit and good jumper is up to taking part in the entry-level divisions. Dressage tests there are uncomplicated, the cross-country courses of not more than a mile or so are inviting (logs, little ditches, and low banks, for example), and the stadium jumping fences are about the size you and Fred did at home.

For Further Information

United States Combined Training Association
525 Old Waterford Road Northwest
Leesburg, VA 20176
phone (703) 779-0440
fax (703) 779-0550
info@eventingusa.com

FOXHUNTING

Mention the word *foxhunting* and most people will respond with something about scarlet-coated 18th-century British gentry galloping after a pack of hounds. These people would be surprised to learn that the sport is very much alive and well in the United States and Canada. There are hunts in just about every state (some, like Virginia and Pennsylvania, have dozens), and you don't have to be a country squire on a 17-hand Thoroughbred to take part.

Hunting isn't all one mad gallop over wooden fences and stone walls. According to its adherents, it's an opportunity to watch a pack of foxhounds try to locate a fox. Of course, the excitement begins when they do and the fox leads them on a chase for miles and miles at a time. (Hounds rarely catch up with or kill their quarry.)

Riding to hounds, as foxhunting is sometimes called, starts in late summer. That's the cubbing season, when young hounds are introduced into the pack. The formal season begins in the fall and lasts until early spring, although some parts of the country stop when winter closes in.

This very formal activity has its own vocabulary and strict code of conduct (no "larking," or unnecessary jumping) and dress (scarlet coats are only for members of the hunt who have earned the right to wear them). However, hunting isn't always as physically demanding as you

Foxhunting is an opportunity to watch hounds try to pick up and then follow a scent.

might think: Some hunts jump fences no higher than 3 feet, and there are often optional routes around jumps. Plus, since hounds don't always pick up a fox's scent, there's plenty of standing around and waiting.

The best way to be introduced to foxhunting is to get in touch with a local hunt club, which you can find out about through your local horse network or the *Chronicle of the Horse* magazine's annual hunting issue.

For Further Information

Masters of Foxhound Association of America
Morven Park
P.O. Box 2420
Leesburg, VA 20177
www.mfha.com

Hunter Pace

Even if the idea of riding to hounds doesn't appeal to you, hunter pacing may. It's an outgrowth of foxhunting that involves completing a 4- to 6-mile cross-country course of jumps in as close to the optimum time as possible (you're not told what that time is). Sometimes the time is set by an experienced rider who completes the course earlier in the week, other times by averaging the times of the competitors.

At intervals of several minutes, teams of two or three riders are sent off to begin the course. The course is well indicated, and in most cases fences are no higher than between 2 and 3 feet. The object is not to race to the finish, but to move at a brisk canter (punctuated by some trotting if you wish) and finish at the optimum time. The closer to that time, the better your score.

For Further Information

Since most hunter paces are sponsored by foxhunts, refer to the information above.

COMPETITIVE TRAIL AND ENDURANCE RIDING

What would you think about taking a 25-mile trail ride? Fifty miles? One hundred miles? That's routine for people who take part in competitive trail rides and endurance rides. And they cover such distances—including up and down hills (sometimes mountains) and across streams—over three days, or two, or even one.

Competitive trail rides are similar to hunter paces: The goal is to cover the distance in as close to a predetermined optimum time as possible; going faster or slower results in penalty points. An endurance ride is more in the nature of a race: The idea is to cover the distance—the most demanding races cover 100 miles—as quickly as possible.

Such physical demands require a sound and well-conditioned horse. As a matter of equine safety, compulsory veterinarian checks occur at the start and end of the day and at stops along the way. The vets and their assistants check pulse and respiration and also look for any sign of stress or lameness. Any horse that doesn't pass muster is eliminated.

As for the people in the saddle, being "riding fit" is essential. A good way to become introduced to competitive trail riding and endurance riding is via novice rides, which may go for only 10 or 15 miles.

Arabians, Morgans, Appaloosas, and cross-breeds containing these breeds have distinguished records in endurance and trail riding. However, other breeds and types have done well, too.

Hint: Dress for comfort and make sure your pants don't chafe.

For Further Information

American Endurance Riding Conference
11960 Heritage Oak, Suite 9
Auburn, CA 95603
phone (530) 823-2260
fax (530) 823-7805
www.aerc.org

POLO

The elitist image of polo may even be stronger than that of foxhunting. Some would say it's deserved, at least with regard to the amount of money required to mount a top-flight international-caliber team; as the saying goes, polo is a disease that can be cured only by poverty.

However, polo is also widely played on a club level, where you don't need to own a string of ponies (the term by which the horses are always referred). In many instances ponies can be rented, especially at the stage where you're learning to play the game.

Outdoor polo has four players on a team. Indoor or arena polo, which uses an inflated ball (outdoor polo uses a solid wooden one), has three players on a side. The game is divided into periods of 7½ minutes known as chukkars. Outdoor polo has eight chukkars, indoor polo six. Because of the pace at which the game is played, players change ponies after every chukkar. The object is to hit the ball through the opponent's goalposts with your long-handled mallet. This parallel to hockey extends to the physicality of both sports. Polo players block shots by hooking an opponent's mallet with their own. They can also drive an opponent off the ball by riding up alongside the other player's pony and pushing against the animal. Because of the potential for serious collisions, rules stipulate who has the right-of-way. Rule violations results in penalty shots.

A brave, agile, and well-schooled pony is essential. Many are Thoroughbreds or Thoroughbred cross-breeds. Players, who also need to have bravery in their résumés, come in all ages, sizes, and both genders.

A bit of trivia: In polo, for safety's sake, all players must hold their mallets in their right hands (the left hand holds the reins).

For Further Information

United States Polo Association
4059 Iron Works Parkway, Suite 1
Lexington, KY 40511-8483
phone (606) 255-0593, (800) 232-USPA
fax (606) 231-9738
www.uspolo.org

THERAPEUTIC RIDING

The effect that riding can have on physically challenged people, with regard to both its therapeutic benefits and the spiritual uplift that contact with horses gives them, is a thing of beauty. Many stables host therapeutic riding programs that are also known as riding for the handicapped. Many of the same horses used for regular lessons take part; how some usually unresponsive animals respond positively to riders who have minimal control is one of life's great wonders.

Therapeutic riding chapters and programs can always use your assistance, whether as a volunteer to lead a horse or walk alongside and support a rider who may need help that way, or financially. Look into it. It's good for the people whom you'll help—and excellent for you and your karma too.

For Further Information

North American Riding for the Handicapped Association
P.O. Box 33150
Denver, CO 80233
phone (800) 369-RIDE (7433), (303) 452-1212
fax (303) 252-4610
fax-on-demand: (303) 457-8496
www.narha.com

14

HORSEBACK VACATIONS

Men are better when riding, more just and more understanding,
and more alert and more at ease and more undertaking, and
better knowing of all countries and of all passages.
—Edward, Duke of York

Thanks to the thriving subcategory of the travel industry known as
equestrian tourism, I've had the opportunity to see a goodly portion of
the world from the saddle over my three decades of writing about horses.
The following "home movies" may strike you as rambling musings, but
they're here to give you an idea of the kinds of domestic and international
vacations that are available.

The wide public pathways that crisscross Spain are called *cañadas*
and were originally used by farmers to take their livestock to market. The
paths are now used as riding trails.

A Spanish horseback holiday organization invited a group of American equestrian journalists to explore Spain along those paths. We met

our hosts and our horses outside of the city of Segovia, north of Madrid. Our guide, a former cavalry officer, exuded Iberian enthusiasm, and the horses seemed happy to be going along, too.

The entourage spent the morning walking and trotting through small villages and past farms. After a stop for lunch and a short rest, we continued along toward our destination for the night, a restored mountain fortress town called Pedraza, which is used as a weekend retreat by Madrid artists and writers.

The entrance to Pedraza was up a cobblestone roadway and under an archway. The sight of centuries-old whitewashed buildings and the sound of hooves on the stones were straight out of every Errol Flynn swashbuckling movie ever made.

The town might have been rustic in feeling but it contained one of Spain's finest restaurants. After a spectacular dinner of roast spring lamb, a sound sleep in private homes, and a fortifying breakfast, we climbed back on our horses the next morning for the return trip (the animals spent the night in a temporary corral). About an hour into the ride we passed through a meadow of wildflowers and herbs. As our horses' hooves crushed the plants, the air was filled with a mélange of spice-rich aromas, the memory of which still lingers.

The Reins In Spain: A herd of equestrian journalists. (credit: Gamecock Photo).

A trip to France included a stay at a 14th-century château in the Cher River valley south of Paris and east of the Loire region. Opened to guests, the castle owned by an elderly marquis who had served with distinction in the Resistance during World War II. The furnishing that surrounded him included a da Vinci portrait, the desk used by Lafayette to write to Louis XVI requesting military assistance for the American colonies, and a piano on which Chopin had dashed off études and waltzes.

The château's restored stables were populated by a dozen horses. Daily rides took us along trails that flanked vineyards and passed through forests where Richelieu's men might have lain in abush for D'Artagnan and his colleagues.

The château's grounds contained a riding ring where I joined the family's youngest generation of riders for a lesson one morning. In the diplomatic words of the instructor, *"Monsieur Price, les coudes, s'il vous plaît"* (rough translation: "We try not to flap our elbows here either").

The broad expanse of Dartmoor is right out of Sherlock Holmes— literally so, because Sir Arthur Conan Doyle lived there when he wrote *The Hound of the Baskervilles*. I had a chance to explore that part of western England during several days of riding out of the archetypically charming village of Widecombe-on-the-Moor.

Moorland is striking in a dour, even harsh way: rolling land covered with sparse grass but abundant gorse and bracken in muted earth tones. Instead of the Baskervilles' hounds, our group came across shaggy and inquisitive wild Dartmoor ponies that followed us in lively canters. Above our heads, clouds swept along in fantastic shapes or gathered to sprinkle us with rain.

Further attractions were rocky outcroppings called tors. Each had a legend attached to it (one summoned up the image of a pack of hounds in pursuit of prey), and as we rode from tor to tor, we took in the sight of fields and villages below stretching toward the horizon and forming patchwork quilts out of the land.

As a certified lesson-head, I seize on vacations as opportunities for concentrated instruction. Most notably, I was one of a group of Americans who spent a week at a combined training facility outside the town of Abergavenny in southern Wales just a few miles from the English border. Since our goal was to take part in a one-day horse trial, the first part of the week was spent learning how to memorize—and ride—a dressage test, negotiate cross-country obstacles, and jump around a course of low stadium jumping fences. (We also learned how to braid our horses' manes: The plaited lumps on my steed's neck resembled a dozen unsightly pompoms). Sarah, the owner of the facility and one of the most perceptive and encouraging instructors on the planet, spent as much time helping us cope with horse-show nerves as she did with matters of position, timing, and pace.

The week's highlight was, of course, the competition. We Yanks took part both as individuals and as members of a U.S. team against squads from England and Wales. To our individual and collective surprise and relief, everyone remembered the dressage test, finished the cross-country course, and left most of the stadium fences up. And to cap off the day, the owner of a neighboring farm who presented the prizes turned out to be the legendary British Olympic show jumper Colonel Sir Harry Llewellyn, who later regaled us with tales of his own competitive experiences winning Olympic medals in 1948 and again in 1952.

Going to Vienna for the World Cup show-jumping finals gave me the opportunity to visit the prominent Spanish Riding School. No, I didn't ride there, but just being a spectator will crown any business or vacation trip to that city. Attending a rehearsal and then a public performance in the baroque riding hall was a quasi-religious experience: Riders in Napoleonic hats and frock coats put the Lipizzaners through their paces to the music of Mozart and Strauss. Especially eye opening are the airs above the ground, movements in which the horses rear and leap.

(Other citadels of classical horsemanship are the Cadre Noir at the French Cavalry School at Saumur and the Royal Andalusian Riding School in Jerez de la Frontera, Spain. All three offer public performances; check schedules and get your tickets well in advance.)

Closer to home, some free time during a trip to Bermuda to cover the island's annual horse show let me try a stable along one of the beaches south of Hamilton. I was boosted onto a Clydesdale, and discovered that until you've cantered some 17 hands above the sand, you just haven't seen all of Bermuda . . . or felt as though you were trapped in a Budweiser commercial.

Not all my adventures have taken me overseas.

I learned to ride as a kid because I wanted to be a cowboy. I wasn't alone. All my friends spent Saturday mornings cheering Roy, Gene, Hoppy, and other six-gun heroes at the movies. At the drop of a ten-gallon hat, we would have gladly given up our Tom Mix secret decoder rings for a chance to join a real posse or cattle drive. However, growing up in New York City and its suburbs made the likelihood of fulfilling such a career dream dubious at best, and I had to wait several decades before I found a treatment for my case of Delayed Cityslicker Syndrome.

I took the cure over a week at a Wyoming guest ranch. In the company of a dozen other guests, I climbed into a Western saddle and did indeed—finally—ride the range. In groups of five or six, we spent mornings and afternoons exploring high meadows and mountain trails; many of us spent nonriding hours fly fishing for native cutthroat trout (hacks and hackles, or tack and tackle, as it were).

Cityslickers: Dude ranching in Wyoming (credit: author).

The wish fulfillment occurred one morning when our trail guide led us to the edge of the ranch's property. There in our path grazed a herd of some 30 cattle. We halted and stared at them. They looked up from their grazing and stared back.

"These cows belong to the reservation on the other side of the hill," our trail guide explained. "They must have escaped. Returning them would be the neighborly thing to do."

Agreeing that it's nice to be neighborly, we fanned out and walked our horses toward the herd. The cattle cooperated by turning and letting us push them along.

Of course we had to sing. Cowboys always sang when they herded cattle—we knew that from the movies. Now, why we started with "golden oldies" rock 'n' roll songs, I'll never know, but that's what we did, and instead of "yippy-ti-yi-yo," the hills were alive to the sound of "doo-wop doo-wop."

On two occasions, a steer slipped out of the herd and ambled away. I took advantage of his independent streak to lope after him, circling around and yahooing him back to the others. At last I had my defining cowboy moment.

On other less wish-fulfilling but no less pleasant outings, I've taken fall foliage trail rides through Vermont and ridden through Virginia's hunt country. Although an hour on an urban park bridle path may not sound much like a real horseback vacation, I've taken advantage of free time and gone riding through New York City's Central Park, Philadelphia's Fairmont Park, Nashville's Percy Warner Park, Los Angeles' Griffith Park, and London's Hyde Park (where the bridle path is called Rotten Row, a corruption of the French words for "the king's route").

I'll end these reminiscences with one of my most memorable junkets.

Thanks to an equestrian travel agency and the Irish Tourist Board, another writer and I spent a week in the horsiest country in the world. My companion was the editor of a prominent equestrian magazine, and we began by spending three days in the Dublin area. One of those days took us to the neighboring county of Wicklow, where our Irish Horse Board host led us on an afternoon's hack that included a glorious gallop across newly mowed turf.

Stopping at a pub on the way back to Dublin gave me another defining moment in my inspired-by-the-movies life. *The Quiet Man* (in a nutshell: John Wayne goes to Ireland) contains a scene in a pub in which a minor character wears riding clothes, smokes a pipe, and quaffs a pint of Guinness. "I could have played that role," I told myself back in my pipe-smoking days when I saw the movie. And at that post-hack pub stop, I looked into the mirror behind the bar and saw myself in boots and breeches, puffing on my pipe and grasping a mug of Stout.

Friday found us on horseback in Limerick, where we were entertained by Thady Ryan, master of the Scarteen Hunt. "And will you join us for a morning's hunting tomorrow?" he wanted to know over lunch. My companion, who was an experienced foxhunter, said she'd be delighted. I declined with thanks. The huge banks and wide ditches that divided the fields in that part of Ireland were well out of my league (at that point in my life, little cross-rails gave me pause for thought).

After lunch a British journalist who had stopped by asked Thady to pose his hounds for a group photo portrait. As the photographer said

Riding along the beach in Ireland. (Photo: Cross Country International).

"cheese," the hounds scented a fox and took off for parts unknown. Within seconds, the stable sprang into action. Horses were tacked, and my colleague and I were given legs-up. Before I knew what was happening, we were galloping after Thady, who was chasing after his hounds, which were chasing after a phantom fox. Over banks and across ditches we galloped. I grabbed mane and prayed. And survived.

The hounds returned to their kennels in their own good time. Thady took our horses, shepherded us into his library, and poured out restorative spirits. "I won't take no for an answer," he said, waving his glass in my direction.

Which is how I got to hunt in Ireland.

Hunting starts early, and the sun was just up when we drove to where the hunt was to begin. I was given a lovely Thoroughbred–Irish draft cross-bred mare to ride. As the Irish description goes, she had the head of a duchess, the hindquarters of a cook, and the manners of a finishing school headmistress. She also had feet the size of dinner plates, all the better to stand up to boggy ground.

For the first two hours we moved from covert to covert (pronounced "cover," it means a likely place to find a fox). The 50 or so riders stood around and waited while Thady's hounds nosed around for quarry. Every now and then we'd encounter a stone wall that had to be jumped, but by the time those of us riding way back got to the obstacle, hooves had turned the wall pretty much into kitty litter.

Then the hounds found a fox and it was off to the races. "You're doing everything you've been told never to do on horseback," I told myself as my mare got caught up in the spirit of the occasion and we cantered down a steep hill, then cantered down a paved road.

When we left the road and jumped into a field, the run began in earnest. Horses scrambled up gorse-covered banks, paused at the top, and then launched across the deep ditches that lay on the other side. Or they leaped ditches onto the sides of banks, which they then scrambled up and leapt off.

After what seemed like hours of breathlessly exhilarating terror, the small group of riders I was following had either the bad luck or the good sense (depending on one's fatigue level) to separate from Thady, his hounds, and the rest of the hunters. We were lost. There was nothing to do

The Not-So-Quiet man: foxhunting in Ireland. (credit: author)

but halt, then walk in the general direction of home. I spent a great deal of time rejoicing in the ability to breathe again and wondering whether the stitch in my side would ever disappear.

Finally we reached the crossroad where the cars and trailers were parked. My companion, who had been with the main group, trotted up and told me how very concerned she had become when she couldn't find me. For all she knew, I was lying in the bottom of a ditch under 3 feet of black water.

Which would have been dreadful, she added, because I was the one who had the car keys.

Before signing up for your first horseback riding vacation, take heed of these few helpful hints:

- Vacations are not the time to break in new boots or other footwear. Wear them at home first and wear them long enough so you're sure they're past the blister-producing stage.
- Take along an extra pair of laces if you wear paddock or field boots, and extra socks.
- People who ride for an hour or two a week won't be accustomed to many hours in the saddle on consecutive days. Pack liniment or

rubbing alcohol, as well as a box of Band-Aids and another of moleskin blister pads.

- If you're staying at a resort or ranch, ask for a list of what clothing is appropriate. Some places couldn't care less about boots and breeches versus chaps. But others do, and you wouldn't want to guess wrong.

- Many ride organizers object to ponchos as rain gear. That's because wind can get under them and make them billow out, which can frighten horses. Rubber or waxed-cotton foul-weather garments are just as effective and potentially safer.

- Be honest when a travel agent and a riding resort or organization asks about your riding skills. Acknowledging that you're a beginner or beginner-intermediate is not only truthful but also sensible. After all, why ask for trouble by being put on a horse that's beyond your capability, especially one you don't know? Besides, the riding staff will see for themselves.

Using a travel agency that specializes in horseback holidays can be of immeasurable help. The following two are gateways to domestic and foreign destinations, including facilities that offer instruction and some of the most exotic spots on the planet. In addition to providing such salient details as dates and prices, their catalogs are fun to savor.

Equitour Fits
Box 807
Dubois, WY 82513
phone (800) 545–0019
fax (307) 455–2354
www.equitour.com.

Cross Country International Equestrian Vacations
P.O. Box 1170
Millbrook, NY 12545
phone (800) 828–8768
fax (914) 677–6077
www.equestrianvacations.com

FOR FURTHER READING

Worldwide Riding Vacations: Rides on 5 Continents by Arthur Sacks
(The Complete Traveler)

Gene Kilgore's Ranch Vacations (John Muir Publications)

Horseback Adventures by Dan Aadland (Howell Book House)

The Whole Horse Catalog by Steven D. Price, editorial director
(Fireside/Simon & Schuster)

15

HORSE CARE

No matter how hungry he may be, [the cowman] takes
care of his horse before looking after his own comfort.
—Ramon Adams, *The Cowman's Code Of Ethics*

Old-timers (that is, anyone who remembers any prior generation)
lament that too many of today's novice riders neither know nor care
about learning horse care. It's said these novices have become accustomed to being waited on. They show up for their lessons and, instead
of first grooming and tacking their horses, they're handed the reins.
Then when they're finished, someone asks, "May I take your horse
from you, please?"

The point is that although knowing how to feed, groom, and
otherwise look after a horse's creature comforts isn't an essential
part of knowing how to ride, it's an essential element of good horsemanship. That's why you should take advantage of every opportunity
to help out with barn chores. Learning about horses from the busi-

ness end of a broom or pitchfork is a honorable pursuit, and you'll find out useful things about equine behavior that books can't even begin to tell you.

FEEDING

Hay

Horses that live in pastures get the nutrients they need from the grass on which they graze. They also have the opportunity for constant grazing, which the equine digestive system is accustomed to. Horses that are deprived of a steady source of fresh or dried grass become prone to digestive ailments, and they also become bored and bad tempered.

Those horses that live in barns must rely on hay, the dried tops and stalks of certain grasses (alfalfa, timothy, and red-tip, to name a few). In addition to nutrients, hay supplies the bulk and roughage necessary for proper digestion.

Bales of hay come apart easily into slices called flakes. Horses usually receive several flakes of hay in the morning and a few more in the afternoon or evening. Some owners make small quantities available in hanging hay nets, which they feel compensates for a stabled horse's inability to graze.

Other owners prefer to feed hay cubes. Cubed hay, which comes in bags, is easy to store and to feed, but it's more expensive than baled hay.

Any hay should be sweet smelling and free of mold and dust. Take a whiff for yourself.

Grain and Feed

Grain supplies energy, which is vital for working horses. Oats provide lots of energy (hence the expression *feeling your oats*), and they're easily digestible. Other grains are corn and bran, the latter being the husks of wheat.

Crushed beet pulp encourages a thin horse to put on weight. The pulp must be thoroughly soaked in water before a horse can digest it.

Feed is composed primarily of grain but with other nutrients and fillers. *Sweet feed* is held together by molasses, which horses find especially palatable. Another kind of feed is squeezed together into pellets. Owners who don't have much storage space tend to favor sweet feed or pellets.

The amount of grain or feed a horse receives depends on his age, his weight, and the amount of work he does. Too much feed, especially oats or corn, can make him too energetic and difficult to ride.

Most horses are fed grain or feed twice a day, once in the morning and again in the late afternoon. Like humans, horses should wait at least a half hour after eating before physical exercise. And after exercise, they should be completely cooled off before eating.

WATER

An adult horse needs a minimum of 8 to 10 gallons of water every day, and more on hot days or after strenuous exercise.

Horses don't like water that's dirty or full of foreign objects. That's why water buckets and tubs must be cleaned on a regular basis.

Some owners like automatic water fountains that refill after the horse has drunk. Others prefer to water by hand so they can monitor the amount the animal has drunk.

As with food, a horse should be thoroughly cool after exercise before being allowed to drink. If not, colic (a severe stomachache) or other medical problems are likely to occur. To determine whether a horse is ready to be put away in his stall, feel his chest between his front legs. If his skin is hot to the touch (in case you're not sure, ask someone), he needs to be walked around until he's cool.

GROOMING

Grooming a horse is more than a cosmetic chore. Brushing and rubbing remove dirt and dried sweat from hair and skin. It's also an opportunity to see whether the animal has any cuts or sores that need attention.

Horses are routinely groomed before being ridden, if for no other reason than to make sure that the hair under his saddle is dirt-free and lying flat so as not to cause saddle sores.

Picking debris out of a horse's foot.

After the horse has been secured by cross-ties or another method, the first step in grooming is to pick out his feet, where dirt, bedding, and small rocks can become lodged. Your instructor or the horse's owner can show you how to lift his feet and hold them up.

A horse secured in cross-ties.

Using a metal hoof pick, scrape from the back of the foot toward the front and between the soft frog and the outside part of the foot. Be especially careful not to scratch the frog with the pick.

Cleaning your horse's feet is a good time to make sure his shoes are on securely.

As for brushing, work from the top of the horse to his feet so you won't have to go back and redo places that you already cleaned.

Rub his neck, his body, and the tops of his legs with a curry comb to loosen any mud and dried sweat. Then use a brush with stiff bristles (called a dandy brush) to clean away any dirt that remains. You can also brush the tail with that tool.

A mane comb is used *only* on the mane, because its hard teeth will break tail hairs. Comb small clumps of hair at a time. Use your fingers to untangle whatever you can't comb away.

Clean your horse's face with a soft brush, being sure to shield his eyes with your nonbrushing hand. You can use that brush to give a final going-over to the rest of his body.

Then wipe around his eyes and nose with a damp sponge.

You don't need to groom your horse this well after you ride him. But you'll still need to brush or sponge away any sweat stains and pick out his feet.

MUCKING OUT

Stall bedding acts as a mattress or carpet. It's more comfortable for a horse to stand on or lie down on than a bare wooden or cement floor would be. Just as important, bedding soaks up moisture from urine and manure.

Among the choices for bedding are straw, wood shavings, or wood sawdust. Many people prefer shavings to sawdust, because the latter forms hard clumps when wet.

Cleaning a stall is called mucking out. How often the chore must be done depends on how much time a horse spends in the stall. As a general rule, people remove manure whenever they see it. That way, the horse has a cleaner stall and the mucker won't have a heavy load at the end of the day.

To muck out a stall, start by moving the horse somewhere else. Pick up the largest pieces of manure with a manure fork and put them in a wheelbarrow. Then dig smaller pieces out of the bedding. Take only the manure and leave as much dry bedding as you can. Add soaked bedding to the wheelbarrow, but spread damp bedding around the stall to dry out. Then empty the wheelbarrow at the manure pile.

Finally, sweep the aisle clean with a broom, pushing any bedding on the floor back into the stall.

One of the highest compliments a horseman can receive is that he or she "keeps a clean barn." That's something to strive for, even if it's not your barn.

The following tips will also help keep horses and barns in good condition:

- Learn to be observant, especially with regard to a horse's behavior. For example, a horse that's sweating and either lying down and writhing in discomfort or nipping at his sides is showing early signs of colic. You'll want to call the barn manager or your instructor without delay. Similarly, a horse that's bleeding or limping or is discharging mucus or pus needs medical attention. When in doubt about whether to summon help, err on the side of caution and notify someone.
- Call your instructor's attention to broken or frayed pieces of tack.
- Even one of a 1,200-plus-pound animal's feet standing on one of yours will bring a tear to the eye. People who wear sneakers, moccasins, or other soft footwear to groom or even lead horses do so at their own risk. Work boots or other hard-toed shoes are highly recommended.
- Dogs belong on leashes and children under supervision whenever they're at a barn.
- Except in designated areas, smoking in a barn is strictly prohibited.

16

FURTHER INFORMATION

By reading, riding and meditating, great results may be obtained, if there
is true feeling for the horse and provided the rider's seat is good.
—Nuno Oliveira, *Reflections on Equestrian Art*

BOOKS

Two good books that are aimed specifically at beginning riders are *Balanced Riding* by Pegotty Henriques (Half Halt Press) and *Riding* by Kate Delano-Condax Decker (The Lyons Press).

Centered Riding by Sally Swift (Trafalgar Square Press) focuses attention on the rider's body position and movement in relation to the horse. Using imaginative metaphors and exercises, the book deserves the great success it has achieved among riders at all levels.

Anyone interested in hunter-seat horsemanship should proceed directly to *Hunter Seat Equitation* by George H. Morris (Doubleday). The preeminent trainer, who has produced decades of Olympic-medal-winning jumper riders after producing decades of equitation champions, shares his expertise in this authoritative textbook that beginners can understand and profit from.

Showing for Beginners by Hallie McEvoy (The Lyons Press) offers basic information about preparing for and taking part in entry-level competitions. It's also a good way to help parents and friends understand what's going on.

Winning with the American Quarter Horse by Don Burt (Doubleday) discusses what Western judges are looking for and, consequently, what's involved in correct rider form and control.

The same value is found in *Winning: A Training and Showing Guide for Hunter Seat Riders* by Anna Jane White-Mullin (Trafalgar Square Press).

Physical fitness is the subject of *Fit to Ride* by Eckart Meyners (Half Halt Press), full of exercises to develop and improve the muscles you use in the saddle.

Fitness, Performance and the Female Equestrian by Mary D. Midkiff (Howell Book House) is full of helpful advice on female physical (including biological) considerations, safety tips, nutritional factors, and other matters of interest to women who ride.

The mental side of riding, especially with regard to staying relaxed and focused during lessons and in the show ring, is addressed in *The Natural Rider* by Mary Wanless and *That Winning Feeling: A New Approach to Riding Using Psychocybernetics* by Jane Savoie (both Trafalgar Square Press).

Reflections on Riding and Jumping by William Steinkraus (Trafalgar Square Press) contains the observations of the Olympic show-jumping individual gold medalist. Although many of the concepts are well beyond the novice stage, the author's insights are worth striving to apply.

An immodest suggestion: *The Whole Horse Catalog,* Steven D. Price, editorial director (Fireside Books/Simon & Schuster), is a sourcebook of equestrian products, services, and organizations.

Equestrian books can be found in tack shops as well as bookstores. The major chains, such as Barnes & Noble, stock a surprisingly large number of horse-related titles, while cyberjockeys might try online bookstores.

Magazines

A popular English-riding how-to monthly, *Practical Horseman* contains instructional articles by many of the country's leading hunter/jumper, dressage, eventing, and endurance/trail riders and trainers. Other areas it covers are stable management and horse health. Detailed photographs accompany the articles' easy-to-follow text.

Horse & Rider is the Western equivalent, with good instructional pieces, too. It comes out every month.

The monthly *Western Horseman* includes how-to articles along with articles on Western lifestyle.

For results and calendars of hunter/jumper, dressage, eventing, and distance/trail competitions, from the local to international level, the weekly *The Chronicle of the Horse* is the magazine of record. It's also the place for news of these disciplines.

Equus, a monthly, focuses on horse health, but there are also items about riding techniques that are of interest to nonowners.

These and other equestrian magazines are available at tack shops and large newsstands. If any strike your fancy, subscription forms are there for the using.

In addition, the activity associations found in chapter 13 publish their own magazines. Many come free with membership in the organization.

VIDEOS

Among good beginner-level instructional tapes are *The Basics of Learning to Ride* by Bob Robinson; *So You Want to Ride a Horse* by Mark Allen; *Beginners Basic System—Introduction to Resistance-Free™ Riding 101* by Richard Shrake; *Centered Riding* by Sally Swift; *The Science of Riding* by George H. Morris; and *Riding and Jumping Techniques* by Bill Steinkraus.

Of particular value to riders at all levels of all disciplines is "Three Masters," a three-volume set that features the legendary hunter/jumper trainer George H. Morris and rider Rodney Jenkins and the well-known exponent of resistance-free training Buck Brannaman (who was the primary inspiration for best-selling novel and film *The Horse Whisperer*).

Filmed over a three-day clinic, the series demonstrates not only how these men develop potential in horses and riders, but how, through the application of experience and "horse sense," horsemanship can be raised to an art as well as a craft.

These and other tapes are sold at tack shops, or you can order them at:

EquiVid
Box 63563, Bandura Highway
Pipe Creek, TX 78063
phone (800) USA-WHOA
www.cybergate.com/horsenet/equivid

THE WEB

There's no lack of horsy sites, some of which will lead to chat groups where you can swap information about riding problems and successes.

www.imh.org will take you to the Kentucky Horse Park's International Museum of the Horse with its 100-plus links. Another popular portal, www.haynet.net, has just about as many links.

In addition, use a search engine under "riding," "horses," or a particular discipline (such as jumping or dressage) and see what's available on any given day.

17

GLOSSARY

action: how a horse moves, especially with regard to how he moves his knees and legs.

aged: said of a horse that is four years or older.

aid: a signal from the rider to the horse, such as leg and **rein** pressure (see **cue**).

amateur: one who rides or drives horses without receiving payment (as distinguished from a professional).

Appaloosa: a breed of horse characterized by a "blanket" of spots on the rump.

Arab: An **Arabian** horse.

Arabian: a breed charactered by fine head and features. **Arabs** are widely used for pleasure riding, showing, and endurance riding.

artificial aid: see **secondary aids.**

back cinch: the rear **girth** of a **Western saddle.**

bar: the space between the horse's incisor and molar teeth in which the **bit** rests in the mouth.

barrel: the midsection of a horse.

bend (verb):   to turn the body laterally, as if bending around the rider's leg. Bending through a turn helps maintain a horse's balance.

billet: a strap on a **saddle** to which the **girth** or **cinch** is buckled.

bit: the mouthpiece portion of a **bridle** to which the **reins** are fastened.

bolt: to run out of control.

bosal (pronounced "bo-SAL"):   a braided rawhide **hackamore** that applies pressure to a horse's nose and chin.

breastcollar: a piece of **tack** that keeps a **saddle** from slipping back.

bridle: a headpiece consisting of a **bit,** straps, and/or **curb chain** to keep the bit in place, and a set of **reins.**

browband: the part of the **bridle** that connects the **cheekpieces** across the horse's forehead.

canter: a three-beat **gait,** a slow or collected **gallop** (known in **Western** riding as **lope**).

cantle: the elevated rear portion of a **saddle.**

cavesson: the noseband of an **English bridle.**

chaps (also pronounced "shaps"):   leather leggings that riders wear for protection and support.

cheekpiece: the portion of a **bridle** that extends along the horse's cheek.

chip: an extra half stride in front of a jump.

cinch: the strap of a **Western saddle** that passes under the horse's belly to hold the saddle in place.

class: an individual event in a horse show.

cluck: a vocal "clicking" by the rider to encourage the horse to move forward.

colic: a painful irritation or blockage of the intestines.

collect: to "gather" or "package" a horse so that the animal's **stride** becomes more compact (see **extend**).

combination: two or three jumps set a total of 40 feet or less apart.

combined training: a sport in which the same horse-and-rider team completes a **dressage** test, covers a cross-country course with unyielding obstacles, and finally jumps a round of show-jumping fences. A combined training competition that takes place over one or two days is a horse trial; one that holds each stage on a successive day is a three-day event.

conformation: an individual horse's physical characteristics in relation to the standards of his particular breed or type.

cooler: a lightweight blanket used after exercise to prevent the horse from catching a chill.

crest: the upper portion of the neck on either side of the mane.

crest release: a jumping technique in which the rider plants his or her hands on the horse's crest during the jump. The crest release supports the rider's upper body and keeps him or her from jabbing the horse's mouth with the **reins**.

crop: a riding whip with a wrist loop at the handle end.

cross-breed: the product of a sire of one breed and a dam of another, such as a Morgan-Arab cross-breed (known as a Morab), and a Thoroughbred-Arab cross-breed (known as an Anglo-Arab).

cross-canter: to canter on one **lead** with the forelegs and the other lead with the hind legs (also known as crossfiring).

cross-rail: a jump composed of two **rails** that form an *X*.

crownpiece: that portion of a **bridle** that goes over the horse's head.

cue: the **Western** term for **aid**, a signal from the rider to the horse.

curb: a **bit** with a **port** and cheek **shanks**, frequently worn by **Western** horses.

curb chain: a chain attached to a curb **bit** and worn behind the horse's jaw to regulate the use of the bit's action.

dam: a horse's mother.

D-ring: any of the D-shaped rings on a **saddle** to which the **latigo** or **breastcollar** is laced or buckled. Also, a variety of **snaffle bit**.

deep: a jumping takeoff spot that's closer to a **fence** than the optimum distance would be. The opposite of **long**.

diagonal: the sequence of footfalls at the **trot**. A rider who moves up and down in the saddle as the horse's left foreleg moves forward and back is **posting** on the left diagonal when the horse is moving clockwise around a ring.

direct rein: **rein** pressure exerted in a straight line from the rider's hand to the horse's mouth.

distance: a colloquial term for the spot from which a horse leaves the ground to jump a **fence** (see **see a distance**, **deep**, and **long**).

dressage (pronounced "dreeh-SAHZE"; French for "training"): the systematic schooling of a horse. Also, a competition in which horses and riders perform a prescribed sequence of movements.

engagement: the technique where in a horse's energy is generated from his **hindquarters** (the phrase is *engaging the hocks*). An engaged horse is so energized that it feels as though he's springing along.

English: referring to a style of riding characterized by a flat, **horn**-less saddle, as distinguished from **Western** riding. Also, the equipment used in this style of riding.

equitation: another word for **horsemanship**.

extend: to encourage a horse to lengthen his **stride** (see **collect**).

fault: a penalty in **jumper classes** for knocking down or refusing to jump an obstacle or for exceeding the time limit.

fence: another word for a jumping obstacle.

fender: the wide panel between the seat and **stirrup** of a **Western saddle**.

flat: riding in a ring without jumping, as in the expression *on the flat*.

flex (verb): to bend the neck longitudinally, as if the horse is touching his chin to his chest.

flying change of lead: a switch of **leads** at the **canter** or **lope** without the horse's breaking **stride** to the **trot** or walk.

forehand: the part of the horse in front of the the **barrel** (see **heavy on the forehand**).

gait: one of the distinctive movements of a horse in motion: the walk, the **trot** or **jog**, the **canter** or **lope**, and the **gallop**.

gallop: the horse's natural four-beat running **gait**.

gelding: a castrated male horse.

girth: the strap that passes under a horse's belly and holds the **saddle** in place.

grade: a horse of mixed breed, an equine "mutt."

green: said of a horse that is untrained or just beginning his training.

ground rail (or **ground pole**): a pole placed on the ground as an obstacle for horses to walk, **trot**, or **canter** over, most often as a training tool for jumping.

gullet: the arched open portion of a **Western saddle** below the **horn** or **pommel**.

hack: a pleasure ride. Also, the informal term for a horse-show under-saddle (that is, with no jumping) **hunter class**.

hackamore: a **bit**-less **bridle** that controls the horse by pressure on his nose.

half-pass: a lateral maneuver in which the horse simultaneously moves sideways and forward.

half-seat: the rider's position in which contact with the horse is only with the lower legs, the rider's seat lifted off the **saddle**. The half-seat (also known as two-point) is used for **cantering** and **galloping**, especially during the approach to a jump.

halt: the position of a horse that is standing still.

hand: the unit by which horses are measured; one hand equals 4 inches. Horses are measured from their **withers** to the ground.

headstall: the part of the **Western bridle** that fits over the horse's head and to which the **bit** is attached.

heavy on the forehand: the expression that describes an unbalanced horse that is carrying too much of his weight on his **forehand**. Horses that are heavy on the forehand lack the ability to move "from behind" or from their hocks with optimum **impulsion**.

hindquarters: the part of the horse behind the **barrel**.

hock: the joint of the hind leg that is the equivalent of a human elbow or knee and provides **impulsion** to move a horse forward.

hold out (verb):   to keep riding along the track on the rail until you're ready to cut into the middle of the ring for your approach to a jump.

hoof: the hard outer portion of the horse's foot.

horn: the upright projection on the front of a **Western saddle**.

horsemanship: the skill of a rider in terms of form and control.

horse trail: see **combined training**.

hunt seat (also called **hunter seat**):   the **English** style of riding based on the position needed for jumping **fences**. So called because of its origins in foxhunting.

hunter: a horse-show division in which horses are judged on their style of moving and jumping ability suitable for the foxhunting field.

impulsion: the way of moving of a horse that uses his hind legs to create the energy to drive his body forward.

in-and-out: a combination of two horse-show jumps set one **stride** apart.

independent seat: a rider's ability to maintain proper position without having to rely on the **reins** for support.

indirect rein: **rein** pressure exerted toward the rider's opposite hand.

irons: a term for **stirrups** on an **English saddle**.

jog: the **Western** term for **trot**, especially a slow **collected** trot.

jump-off: an additional, tie-breaking round in a jumping competition.

jumper: a horse-show division in which horses are scored on their ability to jump **fences** without regard to form or style.

junior: horse-show **classes** for riders under the age of 18.

keeper: the loop in which a strap is put to keep it from flapping, such as on a **bridle**.

knee: the joint in the foreleg between the forearm and cannon bone.

latigo: the strap that fastens the **cinch** on a **Western saddle**.

lead (noun): describing the side on which a foreleg and hind leg precede the other foreleg and hind leg at the **canter** (or **lope**) and **gallop**. A horse moving at those **gaits** is said to be on either the right or left lead (see **cross-canter**).

leading rein: see **opening rein**.

leather: the strap by which the **stirrup** of an **English saddle** is attached.

left behind: the expression for a rider's being thrown back in the **saddle** over a jump, usually because of being behind the horse's balance when the animal leaves the ground.

leg-up: a boost from another person who assists a rider into the **saddle**.

leg-yield (noun): any of the lateral or sideways movements, such as a **side pass**.

long: a jumping takeoff spot that's farther away from the **fence** than the optimum distance would be. The opposite of **deep**.

longe (pronounced and sometimes spelled "lunge"): to exercise a horse by urging him to circle his handler at the end of a rope or canvas or leather longe line attached to the halter or bridle. Being longed is also a way for riders to develop deep and **independent seats**.

lope: a three-beat **gait**, a slow or **collected gallop** (called **canter** in English riding).

lower leg: the rider's leg from calf to anklebone; the part of the leg used to apply **English**-style riding's leg **aids**.

mare: a female horse four years or older, or female horse of any age that has given birth.

martingale: a strap between the horse's forelegs and attached from the **girth** to either the **cavesson** (standing martingale) or the **reins** (running martingale); its purpose is to control excess head movement.

Morgan: a greed of horse that originated in the United States and that is noted for its versatility.

muzzle: the portion of a horse's face between the nostrils and the upper lip.

near side: the left side of a horse.

neck-rein (verb): to apply outside **rein** pressure against the horse's neck in the direction of the turn.

off side: the right side of a horse.

opening (or **leading**) **rein**: the technique of applying **rein** pressure by moving the rein hand out to the side (see **neck-rein**).

oxer: a jumping obstacle made of two or more elements spread apart to give the obstacle width (see **vertical**). The name comes from the type of barriers that kept cattle in fields, since cattle are reluctant to jump over wide fencing.

pelham: a one-piece combination **curb** and **snaffle bit.**

penning: see **team penning**.

pinto: a type of horse marked by patches of white and another color (the appearance is either white with colored patches or a solid color with white patches). Although the word *Paint* is often used interchangeably with *pinto, Paint* properly refers to a registerable breed of horses that is marked the same way.

poll: the highest portion of a horse's head, behind the ears.

pommel: the elevated front portion of an **English** or **Western saddle.**

pony: one of a number of breeds or types of small equines. Technically, any equine that measures under 12.2 **hands** is considered a pony.

port: the arched portion of the mouthpiece of a **curb** or **Pelham bit.**

post (verb): to rise out of and sink back into the **saddle** at the **trot**. Posting makes riding at the trot more comfortable than trying to sit to the **gait.**

primary aids: the rider's legs, hands, seat, and voice.

pulley rein: an "emergency brake" stopping technique in which the rider braces one hand against the horse's **withers** while pulling back and up with the **rein** in the other hand.

Quarter Horse (properly known as the **American Quarter Horse**): a breed most widely used for ranch work, **Western** showing and pleasure riding, and racing. The name comes from its ability to run a quarter of a mile faster than any other breed can.

rail: a term for the poles of which jumps are made. Rails are usually 10 to 15 feet long and have a round or octagonal circumference.

refusal: a horse's stopping in front of a **fence** that the rider intended him to jump. Also called a stop.

reins: the straps extending from the **bridle** to the rider's hands, used to guide the horse's head.

rein-back: the process of asking a horse to back up, or the movement itself.

romal (pronounced "roh-mahl"): a type of **rein** in which the straps coming from the **bit** join into one rein at the point where the rider holds them. Also, the style of riding in which the rider uses such a rein.

run-out: a variety of jumping disobedience in which the horse runs past the **fence** instead of jumping it.

saddle: the piece of **tack** in which a rider sits.

seat: (1) the rider's position in the **saddle**; (2) a specific style of riding, such as **Western stock seat** or **English hunt seat**.

secondary aids: **spurs** and a **crop** (or stick or whip). So called because they reinforce the **primary aids** of the rider's legs, hands, seat, and voice. Also known as **artificial aids**.

see a distance: to estimate where the horse should leave the ground to jump a **fence** (see **deep, long, distance**).

shank: (1) the long leverlike pieces of a **curb bit** to which the **reins** are attached; (2) the rope or strap by which a haltered horse is led (also known as lead shank).

shoulder: the part of the body between the neck and **barrel** to which the forelegs are attached.

shy (verb): to jump sideways as a reaction to being startled.

side pass: a maneuver in which the horse moves to the side with no forward or backward motion.

sire: a horse's father.

skirt: the portion of a **saddle** under a **Western saddle's cantle** or over the **stirrup** bars of an **English saddle**.

snaffle: a **bit** with a straight or jointed mouthpiece and no **port**.

sound: in healthy condition. The word is used especially to describe a horse that is free of any lameness.

split reins: separated, unjoined **reins**.

spurs: metal implements attached to the heels of the rider's boots and used to reinforce the leg **aids**.

stallion: an ungelded male horse of three years or older.

standard: one of the pair of support devices that hold **rails**; a jumping obstacle, or **fence**, is composed of standards and rails.

stirrups: metal or wooden devices in which the rider places his or her feet.

stride: the full length of step at a particular **gait**.

adding a stride: to shorten your horse's stride so that he fits in an extra one between **fences**. For example, if the distance between two fences can be ridden in either four or five strides, to ride it in five strides is said to be adding a stride.

leave out a stride: to lengthen a horse's **stride** so that he takes one fewer between **fences**. For example, if the distance between two fences can be ridden in either four or five strides, to ride it in four strides is said to be leaving out a stride.

stock seat: the formal term for **Western horsemanship**.

tack: a collective term for **saddles, bridles**, and other "horsewear."

tapadero: a leather protection over the front of a Western stirrup.

team penning: a sport in which teams of three riders try to herd three cows into a corral in the fastest time.

Thoroughbred: a breed widely used for racing and **English**-style riding and horse-showing.

three-day event: see **combined training**.

three-point: the position in which the rider's body contact with the horse is with the lower legs and seat. Also known as full seat (see **half-seat**).

throatlatch: the **bridle** strap that buckles under a horse's throat.

tie-down: The **Western** term for a standing **martingale**.

track (noun): the path around the outside edge of a ring or arena, well worn by constant use; (verb) to move in a certain direction, as in "track to the left."

trot: the two-beat **gait** in which the horse's feet move in diagonal pairs (also known as jog).

two-point: see **half-seat**.

two-track: a movement in which the horse moves simultaneously ahead and to the side in an oblique fashion.

unsoundness: an imperfection or a condition, such as lameness, that prevents a horse from being usable.

vertical: any type of jump made of **rails** set one above the others. Unlike an **oxer**, a vertical tests a horse's ability to jump height but not width.

Western: referring to a style of riding based on ranch work and characterized by a **saddle** with a high **pommel** with a **horn** and a high **cantle** (as distinguished from **English** riding). Also, the equipment used in this style of riding.

withers: the highest part of the horse's back, where it meets the neck behind the mane.

INDEX